Creative Cooking

Creative Cooking

EDITED BY
JILL WARNER

THE WARWICK PRESS

Note

It is important to follow *either* the metric *or*
the Imperial measures when using the recipes
in this book.
All spoon measures are level.
Each dish will serve four people, unless
indicated otherwise.
Flour is plain and sugar is granulated,
unless indicated otherwise.

Contents

Soups

Beef Soup with Dumplings

1·7 litres/3 pints water
450 g/1 lb brisket of beef
salt, pepper
1 stick celery
2 carrots
2 leeks
$\frac{1}{2}$ celeriac root, cut into strips
1 tablespoon chopped parsley

DUMPLINGS
300 ml/$\frac{1}{2}$ pint milk
75 g/3 oz butter
salt, pepper, grated nutmeg
100 g/4 oz flour
3 egg yolks
1$\frac{1}{2}$ tablespoons chopped parsley

Bring the water to the boil in a large pan. Add the meat, season with salt, cover the pan, and simmer for 30 minutes, skimming off the fat and any froth from time to time. Tie together the celery, 1 carrot and 1 leek. Add to the pan and continue to simmer, covered, for another 1 hour 20 minutes. Remove the vegetables from the pan and discard. Cut the remaining carrot into strips, and slice the remaining leek.

Add to the soup with the celeriac, season with pepper, cover the pan, and simmer for another 20 minutes.

Meanwhile prepare the dumplings. Put the milk and butter into a pan. Season with salt, pepper and nutmeg, and bring to the boil. Add the flour and stir hard, until the mixture thickens and comes away from the sides of the pan. Remove the pan from the heat. Stir in 1 egg yolk and allow to cool for 5 minutes. Add the remaining egg yolks and 1 tablespoon of the parsley, and mix thoroughly.

Remove the meat from the soup, cut it into cubes and return to the pan. Continue simmering while you form the dumpling mixture into small balls. Add them to the soup. They will rise to the surface when cooked, after about 10 minutes. Serve the soup garnished with the remaining parsley.

Beef soup with dumplings

Veal soup

Oxtail Soup

1 kg/2 lb oxtail
25 g/1 oz lard
100 g/4 oz bacon rind or ham
  scraps
1 onion, chopped
1 stick celery, chopped
1 carrot, chopped
1 leek, chopped
1.5 litres/2½ pints water
300 ml/½ pint white wine
salt

1 bay leaf
5 black peppercorns
3 juniper berries
40 g/1½ oz butter
40 g/1½ oz flour
100 g/4 oz canned mushrooms,
  drained and sliced
1 teaspoon tomato purée
1 tablespoon paprika
4 tablespoons Madeira

Cut the oxtail into pieces 3–5 cm/1¼–2 inches long. Melt the lard in a large saucepan. Add the oxtail pieces and bacon rind or ham scraps, and fry for 15 minutes, until well browned on all sides. Add the onion, celery, carrot and leek, and fry for another 5 minutes. Pour the water and wine into the pan and season with salt. Add the bay leaf, peppercorns and juniper berries. Cover the pan and simmer for 2 hours, skimming off the fat and any froth from time to time. Them remove the pieces of oxtail from the pan, take the meat off the bones and chop it. Put aside. Strain the stock.

  Melt the butter in a pan. Add the flour and fry, stirring, for 5 minutes, until the flour has browned. Gradually stir in the stock. Bring to the boil and simmer for 5 minutes. Add the mushrooms. Mix the tomato purée in a cup with a little of the soup, and then add to the pan. Season to taste with salt, the paprika and the Madeira. Finally, return the meat to the pan and heat through thoroughly before serving.

Veal Soup

225 g/8 oz veal
450 g/1 lb veal bones
1 carrot, chopped
100 g/4 oz celeriac root, chopped
1 onion, sliced
1.5 litres/2½ pints water
40 g/1½ oz butter

40 g/1½ oz flour
40 g/1½ oz ground almonds
1 egg yolk
150 ml/¼ pint single cream
salt, pepper, mild paprika
sugar
sprigs dill

Put the veal, veal bones, vegetables and water into a large saucepan. Bring to the boil, cover, and simmer for 1 hour over gentle heat. Strain the stock. Chop the meat finely and discard the vegetables.

  Melt the butter in a pan, add the flour, and fry for 3 minutes, until golden yellow. Add the stock, bring to the boil and simmer for 5 minutes. Stir in the meat and almonds. Whisk together the egg yolk and cream with 3 tablespoons of the soup. Stir into the pan. Add the seasonings to taste, garnish with the dill and serve.

Pheasant soup

Pheasant Soup

scraps and carcass 1 roast
  pheasant
1 litre/1¾ pints water
1 stick celery, chopped
1 carrot, chopped
1 leek, chopped
salt, pepper
3 juniper berries

50 g/2 oz streaky bacon, chopped
25 g/1 oz flour
200 ml/6 fl oz port
200 g/7 oz canned chanterelle
  mushrooms, drained
2 tablespoons single cream
1 tablespoon chopped parsley

Cut the pheasant meat into even-sized strips and put aside.
Put the carcass into a large saucepan, add the water and bring
to the boil. Add the celery, carrot and leek, and season with
salt. Tie the juniper berries in muslin and add to the stock.
Reduce the heat and simmer, covered, for 30 minutes.

In another saucepan, fry the bacon gently until the fat runs.
Sprinkle on the flour and allow to brown. Strain the pheasant
stock into the pan. Add the port and season with pepper.
Then add the strips of pheasant meat and the mushrooms,
and simmer for another 5 minutes. To serve, transfer the soup
to a warmed tureen, pour on the cream and garnish with the
chopped parsley.

Cock-a-leekie Soup

1 kg/2 lb boiling chicken
1·7 litres/3 pints water
salt, pepper, grated nutmeg

450 g/1 lb leeks, sliced
100 g/4 oz prunes, soaked and
  drained

Put the chicken into a large saucepan. Add the water and
bring to the boil. Skim off any froth or bits that rise to the
surface. Season with salt, pepper and nutmeg, and simmer,
covered, for 1 hour. Then add half the leeks and simmer, still
covered, for another hour.

Remove the chicken from the stock and cut off the meat.
Reserve the best pieces for another recipe, and cut the
remainder into narrow strips. Put the pieces of chopped
chicken, the prunes and the remaining leeks into another pan.
Strain on the stock, bring to the boil, cover, and simmer for a
further 30 minutes. Adjust seasoning and serve.

Pea soup with gammon

Pea Soup with Gammon

450 g/1 lb dried yellow peas
1·5 litres/2½ pints water
3 onions
3 cloves
salt

450 g/1lb smoked gammon
1 teaspoon dried marjoram
1 teaspoon dried thyme
sprig parsley

Soak the peas overnight in the water.

To make the soup, finely chop 2 of the onions. Leave the remaining onion whole, and stick the cloves into it. Put the peas and the soaking water into a large pan. Salt lightly and bring to the boil. Add the onions and simmer for 20 minutes. Then add the meat, marjoram and thyme, bring back to the boil, and simmer, covered, for a further 1 hour 40 minutes.

Remove the whole onion from the pan and discard. Take out the meat and cut it into thick slices. Season the soup to taste with salt. To serve, pour the soup into a bowl and lay the slices of meat on top. Garnish with the parsley.

Scotch Broth

450 g/1 lb scrag neck of mutton
1·7 litres/3 pints stock
salt, pepper
2 carrots, sliced
1 small turnip, chopped
2 leeks, sliced

40 g/1½ oz pearl barley
2 lumps sugar
600 g/1¼ lb small potatoes, peeled
tarragon vinegar
1 tablespoon chopped parsley

Cut the meat into cubes 3 cm/1¼ inches large. Bring the stock to the boil in a large pan, add the meat and season generously. Cover the pan and simmer very gently for 1 hour, skimming the fat off the surface from time to time.

Add the carrots, turnip, leeks, pearl barley and sugar, and continue to simmer gently, still covered, for 1½ hours. Then add the potatoes and simmer for a further 30 minutes.

Season with a little tarragon vinegar, and more salt if necessary. Garnish with the parsley and serve.

Scotch broth

Fish soup

Fish Soup

2 onions	salt
1·2 litres/2 pints water	1 tablespoon oil
1 stick celery, chopped	50 g/2 oz streaky bacon, chopped
1 carrot, chopped	1 tablespoon flour
1 leek, chopped	150 ml/¼ pint soured cream
1 bay leaf	20 g/¾ oz horseradish, grated
5 white peppercorns	2 potatoes, boiled in their skins
5 allspice berries	1 tablespoon chopped parsley
300 g/10 oz fillet of cod	

Cut 1 onion into quarters. Finely chop the second onion and set aside. Bring the water to the boil in a large saucepan. Add the quartered onion, the celery, carrot, leek and the spices. Reduce the heat, cover, and simmer for 15 minutes. Then season the fish with salt, add to the vegetable stock and poach for 15 minutes, until done.

While the fish is poaching, heat the oil in a second saucepan. Add the bacon and fry gently for 5 minutes. Add the finely chopped onion and fry for 3 minutes, until pale yellow. Stir in the flour and fry until light brown. Remove the fish from the stock, and strain the stock into the pan containing the bacon, onion and flour. Bring to the boil and simmer for 10 minutes.

Meanwhile, stir the cream into the horseradish. Peel the cooked potatoes and cut into small dice. Cut the fish into 2 cm/¾ inch pieces. Add all three to the soup and heat through. Serve garnished with the parsley.

Cream of Leek Soup

600 ml/1 pint water	25 g/1 oz flour
450 g/1 lb leeks, sliced	juice ½ lemon
1 small onion, finely chopped	150 ml/¼ pint single cream
salt, grated nutmeg	1 egg yolk
sugar	1 tablespoon chopped chives
25 g/1 oz butter	

Bring the water to the boil in a large pan. Add the leeks and onion, and season with salt, nutmeg and sugar. Cover the pan and simmer for 30 minutes. Drain, reserving the stock. Sieve the leeks and onion, or process in an electric blender. Keep the stock and purée hot.

Melt the butter in a pan, sprinkle on the flour, and fry for 3 minutes, stirring. Still stirring, add the reserved stock and the leek and onion purée. Bring to the boil and simmer for 5 minutes. Then stir in the lemon juice. Mix the cream and egg yolk in a cup. Remove the pan from the heat and stir in the cream and egg mixture. Heat through gently and adjust the seasoning if desired. To serve, pour the soup into 4 warmed bowls and garnish with the chives.

Cream of Mushroom Soup

300 g/10 oz button mushrooms
50 g/2 oz butter
1 small onion, finely chopped
20 g/¾ oz flour
1.5 litres/2½ pints stock
salt, pepper
150 ml/¼ pint single cream
2 egg yolks
1 teaspoon lemon juice
1 tablespoon chopped parsley

Put aside a few of the smallest mushrooms for the garnish. Finely slice the remainder. Melt the butter in a pan, add all the mushrooms and the onion, and fry gently for 5 minutes. Remove the small whole mushrooms from the pan, set aside and keep warm. Sprinkle the remaining mushrooms and onion with the flour, and stir well. Then add the stock gradually, stirring all the time. Bring to the boil, season, and simmer over gentle heat for 15 minutes.

Beat the cream and egg yolks together. Remove the pan from the heat, stir in the cream and egg yolk mixture, and reheat gently without boiling. Remove the pan from the heat again, and stir in the lemon juice.

To serve, pour the soup into 4 warmed soup bowls and garnish with the whole mushrooms and the parsley.

Cream of Mushroom Soup with Ham

2 cans cream of mushroom soup
   (418 g/14¾ oz each)
200 g/7 oz canned button
   mushrooms
4 slices lean cooked ham,
   chopped
2 egg yolks
4 tablespoons grated
   Emmenthal cheese
4 sprigs parsley

Reheat the mushroom soup according to the instructions on the cans. Add the mushrooms, with their liquid, and the ham. Heat through gently for 5 minutes. Lightly whisk the egg yolks with a little of the soup, and then add to the pan. Reheat to just below boiling point. To serve, pour the soup into 4 warmed soup bowls, sprinkle 1 tablespoon of cheese over each, and garnish with the parsley sprigs.

Cream of Mushroom Soup with Shrimps

50 g/2 oz butter
300 g/10 oz button mushrooms,
   finely sliced
salt, pepper
25 g/1 oz flour
500 ml/18 fl oz stock
500 ml/18 fl oz water
150 ml/¼ pint single cream
200 g/7 oz canned shrimps
1½ tablespoons sherry
1 teaspoon chopped fresh dill
   or ½ teaspoon dried dill
2 tablespoons chopped parsley

Melt the butter in a pan. Add the mushrooms and fry gently for 5 minutes. Season with pepper. Sprinkle on the flour, stirring thoroughly. Gradually stir in the stock and water. Bring to the boil, cover, and simmer gently for 10 minutes. Remove the pan from the heat, stir in the cream, and season to taste with salt. Add the shrimps with any liquid from them, the sherry, dill and 1 tablespoon of the parsley. Reheat to just below boiling point. To serve, pour the soup into 4 warmed soup bowls and garnish with the remaining parsley.

French Onion Soup

40 g/1½ oz butter
300 g/10 oz onions, sliced
2 cloves garlic, chopped
20 g/¾ oz flour
1.5 litres/2½ pints hot stock
salt, pepper
4 thick slices French bread
100 g/4 oz Gruyère cheese,
   grated

Melt the butter in a saucepan, and fry the onions and garlic until pale yellow. Sprinkle on the flour and cook gently, stirring, for 5 minutes. Add the stock to the pan, season, stir well and simmer over gentle heat for 20 minutes.

Toast the slices of bread. Sprinkle the cheese over the bread and grill until melted. Pour the hot soup into 4 warmed soup bowls and place 1 cheese croûton in each bowl. Serve immediately.

From top to bottom: cream of mushroom soup, cream of mushroom soup with ham, cream of mushroom soup with shrimps

Semolina soup

Semolina Soup

60 g/2½ oz semolina
25 g/1 oz butter
2 carrots, diced
¼ celeriac root, diced

1 leek, sliced
1·5 litres/2½ pints hot stock
salt, pepper
1 tablespoon chopped parsley

Put the semolina in a pan. Stir over gentle heat for 2 minutes, until lightly browned. Add the butter and the vegetables, and fry for 10 minutes, stirring, until the vegetables are browned. Add the stock, bring to the boil, and simmer for 10 minutes. Season to taste, garnish with the parsley and serve.

Cheddar Cheese Soup

25 g/1 oz butter
2 onions, finely chopped
3 carrots, chopped
2 green peppers, seeded and chopped
1·5 litres/2½ pints hot chicken stock

25 g/1 oz flour
300 ml/½ pint milk
225 g/8 oz Cheddar cheese, grated
2 canned celery hearts, drained and finely sliced
salt, pepper

Melt the butter in a pan. Add the onions, carrots and peppers, and fry gently for 5 minutes. Pour in the hot stock, bring to the boil, and simmer over gentle heat for 10 minutes. Separately, blend the flour into the milk until smooth, and then stir into the soup. Bring back to the boil and simmer for 5 minutes. Sprinkle on the cheese, and allow it to start melting, stirring all the time. Add the celery and season to taste. Serve immediately in 4 warmed soup bowls.

Pâtés and Savoury Pastries

Pâtés and Savoury Pastries

Liver Pâté

150 g/5 oz white bread, crusts
  removed
400 ml/¾ pint milk
300 g/10 oz pig's liver
150 g/5 oz tender veal
150 g/5 oz unsmoked bacon
1 small onion, quartered

1 tablespoon chopped parsley
2 tablespoons brandy
2 eggs, lightly beaten
salt, pepper, dried marjoram
150 g/5 oz pork back fat, very
  thinly sliced

Soak the bread in the milk for 15 minutes. Meanwhile trim all tubes and remnants of membrane from the liver, and pat dry with absorbent paper.

Squeeze out the bread. Put it twice through the finest blade of the mincer with the liver, veal, bacon and onion. Place the minced ingredients in a bowl. Add the parsley, brandy and eggs, and season with salt, pepper and marjoram. Mix well. Line the base and sides of a terrine or rectangular cake tin with two-thirds of the fat. Put the pâté mixture into the terrine or cake tin, and smooth the top. Cover with the remaining slices of fat. Place in a roasting pan half filled with water, and bake at 200°C/400°F/gas 6 for 1¼ hours. Remove from the oven and allow to cool. Turn out on to a dish and cut in slices for serving.

Liver pâté

Hare Pâté

50 g/2 oz lard
1 kg/2 lb hare portions, skinned, boned and chopped
1 stick celery, chopped
1 carrot, chopped
1 leek, chopped
1 tablespoon chopped parsley
2 tablespoons brandy
100 g/4 oz smoked pork back fat, chopped
1 large onion, sliced
2 tablespoons Madeira
salt, pepper
1 teaspoon mild paprika
1 teaspoon dried marjoram
150 g/5 oz pork back fat, very thinly sliced

Melt the lard in a pan and fry the hare meat, celery, carrot, leek and parsley for 15 minutes, until the meat is browned all over. Pour in the brandy and let the liquid boil away. Transfer the mixture to a bowl.

Gently fry 2 tablespoons of the smoked fat in a pan until the fat runs; keep the rest of the fat aside. Fry the onion in the fat for 10 minutes, until light brown. Add to the meat mixture with the Madeira. Mix well, and put twice through the finest blade of the mincer. Return to the bowl and mix in the remaining smoked fat. Season with salt, pepper, the paprika and marjoram; the pâté should be highly seasoned. Mix together thoroughly.

Use the sliced fat to line the base and sides of a terrine or rectangular cake tin. Put in the pâté mixture, smooth the top and cover with aluminium foil. Bake at 220°C/425°F/gas 7, on the bottom shelf of the oven, for 45 minutes. Remove the foil 10 minutes before the end of the cooking time. Take the dish out of the oven. Turn the pâté out on to a plate or a wooden board, and allow to cool. Cut the pâté into slices and serve with cranberry sauce.

Hare pâté

Rabbit terrine

Rabbit Terrine

2 kg/4 lb rabbit, ready to cook
salt, pepper, cayenne, mild
 paprika, dried thyme
250 ml/8 fl oz brandy
½ white bread roll, crusts
 removed
150 ml/¼ pint warm milk
3 shallots, finely chopped
1 clove garlic, finely chopped

225 g/8 oz continental veal
 sausage, if available
1 rabbit liver
1 egg, lightly beaten
200 g/7 oz pork back fat, very
 thinly sliced
3 bay leaves
1 sprig fresh thyme

Cut the fillets of meat from the back and hind legs of the
rabbit with a sharp knife. Place them in a bowl, season with
salt and pepper, and pour over the brandy. Cover and leave to
marinate for 1½ hours.

Cut the bread roll into small pieces and soak in the milk for
15 minutes. Put the shallots and garlic into a bowl. Squeeze
out the bread and add to the shallots and garlic. Remove the
rest of the meat from the rabbit carcass and chop finely. Add
to the bowl. Cut the veal sausage in half lengthways, take out
the filling and add to the bowl. (If you find veal sausage is
unobtainable, substitute the same quantity of another firm

sausage, or sausage meat.) Trim all tubes and remnants of
membrane from the liver, cut it into quarters, and add to the
bowl. Put the contents of the bowl twice through the finest
blade of the mincer. Season with salt, pepper, cayenne,
paprika and dried thyme.

Take the rabbit fillets out of the marinade, drain and set
aside. Add the marinade and the egg to the minced ingredients
and mix well.

Line the base and sides of a terrine or ovenproof dish with
two-thirds of the fat. Add half of the minced mixture, then the
rabbit fillets, and then the rest of the minced mixture.
Arrange the remaining slices of fat over the top and press
down well. Lay the bay leaves and the sprig of fresh thyme on
top of the fat. Put a lid on the dish, place in a roasting pan
half filled with water, and bake at 220°C/425°F/gas 7, on the
bottom shelf of the oven, for 1 hour 20 minutes. Remove from
the oven and serve hot or cold. If serving cold, allow to cool
without removing the lid.

Goose liver pâté

Goose Liver Pâté

600 g/1¼ lb goose livers
25 g/1 oz canned truffles, drained and thinly sliced
4 tablespoons Madeira
4 tablespoons brandy
salt, pepper, dried thyme
½ bay leaf

2 onions, quartered
450 g/1 lb belly of pork
2 eggs, lightly beaten
25 g/1 oz breadcrumbs
1 tablespoon chopped parsley
150 g/5 oz pork back fat, very thinly sliced

Trim all tubes and remnants of membrane from the livers, and pat them dry with absorbent paper. Put them in a bowl, and arrange the truffles on top. Mix together the Madeira and brandy, and season with salt, pepper, a pinch thyme and the half bay leaf. Pour this mixture carefully over the livers and truffles and leave to marinate, covered, for 12 hours.

Remove the livers from the marinade and drain well. Chop the sliced truffles into matchsticks, and spike the livers on them. Set aside. Put the onions and pork twice through the finest blade of the mincer, and mix in a bowl with the eggs and breadcrumbs. Mix in the parsley and adjust the seasoning to taste.

Line the base and sides of a terrine or rectangular cake tin with two-thirds of the fat. Put half of the minced mixture into the terrine or cake tin, smoothing it level. Place the truffles and livers on top, and cover with the remaining minced mixture. Arrange the rest of the sliced fat over the top. Place in a roasting pan half filled with water, and bake at 200°C/400°F/gas 6, on the bottom shelf of the oven, for 1½ hours. Remove from the oven and allow to cool. Turn out on to a dish and cut in slices for serving.

Spinach Tart

SERVES 6

125 g/4½ oz butter
250 g/9 oz flour
salt
1 egg
1 kg/2 lb spinach, washed and picked over

200 g/7 oz streaky bacon
1 tablespoon chopped parsley
2 cloves garlic
100 g/4 oz Parmesan cheese, grated

To make the pastry, melt the butter in a pan and allow to cool. Sift the flour and a pinch of salt into a bowl. Make a well in the centre and break the egg into it. Scatter the cooled butter around the edge of the flour. Work the ingredients together quickly, working from the outside in, until you have a smooth dough. Shape into a ball, cover, and leave in the refrigerator for 1 hour before use.

Put the spinach into a pan without any water, salt it and bring to the boil. Squeeze out all moisture and chop finely, or put through the fine blade of the mincer. Set aside. Chop half the streaky bacon and fry for 5 minutes in a pan. Add the parsley and garlic and fry for 2 minutes. Add the spinach, cover, and cook very gently for another 5 minutes. Take out the garlic cloves. Remove the pan from the heat, mix in the cheese and allow to cool.

Grease a 25 cm/10 inch loose-based or spring clip tin. Roll out just over half the pastry on a lightly floured surface, and use to line the tin. Fill with the spinach mixture. Roll out the remaining pastry and use to cover the tart, pressing the edges together firmly. Bake at 200°C/400°F/gas 6 for 50 minutes. After 30 minutes cover the top of the tart with the remaining bacon rashers. Remove from the oven and serve hot.

Veal and ham pie

Veal and Ham Pie

SERVES 6

250 g/9 oz flour
salt, pepper
3 tablespoons white wine
150 g/5 oz butter or lard, cut into pieces
400 g/14 oz ham, thinly sliced
400 g/14 oz leg of veal, thinly sliced
6 shallots, chopped
200 g/7 oz mushrooms, thinly sliced
2 tablespoons chopped parsley
250 ml/8 fl oz meat stock
1 egg yolk
1 tablespoon milk
3 leaves gelatine
$\frac{1}{2}$ teaspoon meat extract

To make the pastry, sift the flour and a pinch of salt into a bowl. Make a well in the centre and pour the wine into it. Scatter the fat round the edge of the flour. Work the ingredients together quickly, working from the outside in, until you have a smooth dough. Shape into a ball, cover, and leave in the refrigerator for 30 minutes before use.

Generously grease a 28 cm/11 inch pie dish with margarine. Put a layer of ham on the bottom, then a layer of veal, then a layer of shallots and mushrooms. Season lightly with salt and pepper and sprinkle with a little chopped parsley. Continue layering the ingredients, finishing with a layer of ham. Pour half the stock over the top.

Roll out the pastry on a lightly floured surface to a thickness of 3 mm/$\frac{1}{8}$ inch. Cut out a circle slightly larger than the pie dish. Cut two-thirds of the remaining pastry into a strip, and place around the edge of the pie dish. Beat together the egg yolk and milk, and paint the pastry strip with it. Cover the pie with the pastry lid, pressing the edges well together. Cut a hole in the centre of the pie crust to let out the steam and glaze the pastry with the egg yolk and milk. Cut the remaining scraps of pastry into decorative shapes, place on top of the crust, and glaze them. Bake at 200°C/400°F/gas 6 for 1 hour. Remove from the oven and allow to cool while making the aspic jelly.

Wash the gelatine leaves in cold water, and then soak them in a bowl of cold water for 15 to 20 minutes, until soft. Lightly squeeze out any surplus water, and place the gelatine in a clean bowl. Add the remaining stock and the meat extract. Place the bowl in a pan of hot water and heat gently, stirring, until the gelatine has dissolved. Do not allow to boil. Pour the liquid into the pie through the hole in the centre, and place in the refrigerator to set. Serve cold.

Ham and cheese flan

Celery Flan

SERVES 8

300 g/10 oz flour
salt, pepper
60 g/2½ oz lard, cut into pieces
60 g/2½ oz butter, cut into pieces
3–4 tablespoons water

600 g/1¼ lb sticks celery, chopped
6 eggs
100 g/4 oz Parmesan cheese,
  grated
2 onions, chopped

To make the pastry, sift the flour and a good pinch of salt into a bowl. Scatter in the fats, and rub them in with the fingertips until the mixture resembles fine breadcrumbs. Sprinkle on the water, and mix in lightly with a palette knife until the mixtures leaves the sides of the bowl. Gather the dough into one piece and knead lightly on a floured surface until free from cracks. Chill for 30 minutes before use. Roll out the pastry on a floured surface and use to line a 30 cm/12 inch flan case. Set aside while you make the filling.

Bring a pan of salted water to the boil, add the celery and boil for 5 minutes. Drain. Beat the eggs and cheese together in a large bowl. Stir in the celery and onions, and season well. Pour the mixture into the flan case and smooth the top. Bake at 220°C/425°F/gas 7 for 40 minutes, until the filling is set and the pastry lightly browned. Remove the flan from the oven and serve immediately.

Ham and Cheese Flan

SERVES 6

PASTRY
200 g/7 oz flour
salt
1 egg
90 g/3½ oz butter, cut into pieces

FILLING
200 g/7 oz Emmenthal cheese,
grated

3 eggs, separated
30 g/1¼ oz flour
250 ml/8 fl oz soured cream
salt, grated nutmeg
200 g/7 oz lean cooked ham,
  chopped

To make the pastry, sift the flour and a pinch of salt into a bowl. Make a well in the centre and break the egg into it. Scatter the butter round the edge of the flour. Work the ingredients together quickly, working from the outside in, until you have a smooth dough. Shape into a ball, cover, and leave in the refrigerator for 30 minutes before use.

To make the filling, mix together the cheese, egg yolks, flour and cream until thick and smooth. Season with salt and nutmeg. Grease a 23 cm/9 inch loose-based or spring clip tin. Roll out the pastry on a lightly floured surface and use to line the tin. Beat the egg whites until stiff, and fold them into the cheese mixture. Place the ham over the pastry base and pour the cheese mixture on top. Bake at 200°C/400°F/gas 6 for 30 minutes. Remove from the oven and serve immediately on a warmed plate.

Onion flan

Onion Flan

SERVES 6

250 g/9 oz flour

salt, pepper, paprika, ground
  cumin

250 g/9 oz curd cheese

150 ml/¼ pint water

100 g/4 oz butter

8 large onions, chopped

300 ml/½ pint single cream

150 ml/¼ pint yogurt

3 eggs

1 tablespoon cornflour

To make the pastry, sift the flour and a pinch of salt into a mixing bowl. Crumble in the cheese, and use the fingertips to rub it into the flour. Add the water and knead all together to make a smooth dough. Wrap in greaseproof paper, and allow to rest for 1 hour in the refrigerator.

Melt the butter in a pan and fry the onions gently until transparent but not too soft. Remove from the pan and allow to cool. Meanwhile line a deep 20 cm/8 inch loose-based or spring clip tin with greased greaseproof paper. Roll out the pastry on a lightly floured surface and use to line the tin.

Spread the onions evenly over the pastry. Beat together the cream, yogurt, eggs, seasonings and cornflour, and pour over the onions. Bake at 230°C/450°F/gas 8 on the bottom shelf of the oven, for 25 minutes. When the filling is set and the pastry cooked, remove the flan from the tin and place on a flat plate or board. Serve while still hot.

Leek Pie

SERVES 6

300 g/10 oz puff pastry
1·25 kg/2¾ lb leeks, sliced
50 g/2 oz butter
20 g/¾ oz flour

150 ml/¼ pint single cream
salt, pepper, grated nutmeg
2 egg yolks

Grease a 25 cm/10 inch loose-based or spring clip tin. Roll out half the pastry on a lightly floured surface and use to line the tin. Put on the bottom shelf of the oven and bake blind, at 200°C/400°F/gas 6, for 15 minutes.

Meanwhile, make the filling. Bring a pan of salted water to the boil and blanch the leeks for 2 minutes. Drain thoroughly. Melt half the butter in a pan, add the leeks and stew, covered, for 10 minutes. Melt the remaining butter in another pan, add the flour, and fry gently, stirring, for 2 minutes. Stir in the cream little by little, and simmer gently for 4 minutes. Season the sauce well with salt, pepper and nutmeg. Remove the pan from the heat. Mix 1 egg yolk with a little of the sauce in a cup, then add to the pan, stirring. Add the leeks, with the butter and juices in which they were cooking, and mix thoroughly. Allow to cool.

Put the leek mixture into the half-baked case. Roll out two-thirds of the remaining pastry on a lightly floured surface into a circle slightly larger than the tin. Cut the remaining pastry into a strip and place around the edge of the tin, pressing on firmly. Cover the filling with the pastry circle, and make decorative shapes for the top from any pastry bits left over. Prick the pastry several times with a fork. Beat the remaining egg yolk and use to glaze the pie. Place on the bottom shelf of the oven and bake at 200°C/400°F/gas 6 for 40 minutes. Remove from the oven and serve hot.

Above: leek pie

Cheese Slices

300 g/10 oz puff pastry
250 ml/8 fl oz milk
250 ml/8 fl oz single cream
4 eggs, beaten
350 g/12 oz Emmenthal cheese, grated

3 tablespoons chopped parsley
1½ tablespoons chopped dill
40 g/1½ oz flour
1 tablespoon celery salt
pepper, grated nutmeg

Grease a baking sheet 30 × 40 cm/12 × 15¾ inches. Roll out the pastry on a lightly floured surface and use to line the sheet. Prick the pastry with a fork.

Mix together the milk, cream and eggs. Stir in the cheese, herbs, flour and seasonings. Spread this mixture evenly over the pastry and then allow to rest for 10 minutes. Bake at 200°C/400°F/gas 6 for 40 minutes. Allow to cool slightly, then cut into slices for serving.

Cheese slices

Egg and Bacon Flan

SERVES 6

225 g/8 oz flour
salt, pepper, grated nutmeg
4 eggs
100 g/4 oz butter, cut into pieces

150 g/5 oz lean bacon
250 g/9 oz Emmenthal cheese,
  thinly sliced

To make the pastry, sift the flour and a pinch of salt into a mixing bowl. Make a well in the centre and break in 1 egg. Scatter the butter round the edge of the flour. Working from the outside in, rub the ingredients together with the fingertips to make a smooth dough. Form into a ball, wrap in greaseproof paper, and allow to rest for 30 minutes in the refrigerator before use.

Grease a 25 cm/10 inch loose-based or spring clip tin. Roll out the pastry on a lightly floured surface and use to line the tin. Prick the base several times with a fork.

To make the filling, blanch the bacon by putting it in a bowl and pouring boiling water over it. Leave to stand for 3 minutes, then drain and dry it. Remove the rind and any gristle, and cut into small pieces. Cover the base of the flan with some of the bacon pieces, followed by a layer of cheese slices. Continue layering the bacon and cheese alternately, until all used up. Beat the remaining eggs in a separate bowl and season with salt, pepper and nutmeg. Pour on top of the cheese and bacon layers. Bake at 200°C/400°F/gas 6 for 25 minutes.

When the filling is set and the pastry is cooked, remove the flan from the tin and place on a flat plate or board. Serve while still hot.

Egg Patties

MAKES 12

50 g/2 oz butter
1 onion, chopped
200 g/7 oz mushrooms, chopped
salt, pepper, grated nutmeg
1 tablespoon flour

150 ml/¼ pint single cream
1 tablespoon chopped parsley
3 hard-boiled eggs, chopped
300 g/10 oz puff pastry
1 egg, beaten

Melt the butter in a pan and fry the onion until it is beginning to soften. Add the mushrooms, season with salt and pepper, and cook gently over low heat for 10 minutes, until all the moisture has evaporated. Mix the flour and cream together until smooth, and stir into the mushroom mixture. Simmer gently for 5 minutes. Stir in the parsley and hard-boiled eggs, season with nutmeg, and allow to cool.

Roll out the pastry thinly on a lightly floured surface. Using a 12 cm/4¾ inch notched pastry cutter, cut out 12 rounds. Paint them with cold water. Divide the filling between them, placing a spoonful on one half of the circle, and folding the other half over it. Press the edges well together. Paint the patties with the beaten egg, and place them on a greased baking sheet. Bake at 200°C/400°F/gas 6 for 25 minutes. Remove from the oven and serve hot.

Left: egg and bacon flan
Below: egg patties

Artichoke Flan

SERVES 8

PASTRY

250 g/9 oz flour
salt
1 egg
2 tablespoons grated Parmesan
  cheese
150 g/5 oz butter, cut into pieces

FILLING

750 g/1½ lb canned artichoke
  hearts

milk as required
20 g/¾ oz butter
30 g/1¼ oz flour
salt, pepper, grated nutmeg
2 tablespoons grated Parmesan
  cheese
2 egg yolks

To make the pastry, sift the flour and a pinch of salt into a bowl. Add the egg, and scatter in the cheese and butter. Work the ingredients together quickly, using the fingertips, to form a smooth dough. Shape into a ball, cover, and leave for 30 minutes in the refrigerator before use.

Meanwhile, prepare the filling. Drain the artichoke hearts, reserving the liquid. Make it up to 250 ml/8 fl oz with milk. Melt the butter in a pan, sprinkle on the flour, and fry gently, stirring, for 2 minutes. Pour in the measured liquid. Bring slowly to the boil, stirring continuously. Simmer for 7 minutes, stirring occasionally. Remove the pan from the heat and season the sauce with salt, pepper and grated nutmeg. Stir in the cheese. Mix a little of the sauce into 1 of the egg yolks, and then return to the pan. Cut the artichoke hearts into even slices. Stir into the sauce and allow to cool.

To assemble the flan, roll out half the pastry on a lightly floured surface. Using a 5 cm/2 inch notched pastry cutter, cut out 37 circles. Oil a 25 cm/10 inch loose-based or spring clip tin. Place the circles in it, over the base and sides, in overlapping layers; there should be no gaps left between them. Roll out half the remaining pastry and use to line the tin, covering the circles. Put the filling into the pastry case and smooth the top. Roll out the remaining pastry and use to cover the filling. Bake at 180°C/350°F/gas 4 for 45 minutes.

Remove the flan from the oven and allow to cool in the tin. Invert on to a wire rack. Beat the remaining egg yolk in a cup, and use it to glaze the flan before serving. Reheat for 10 minutes at the same temperature as before. Take the flan out of the oven, slide it on to a warmed plate and serve.

Artichoke flan

Fish

Fish

Windsor Herrings

4 herrings, scaled, cleaned and boned
juice 1 lemon
salt
4 tablespoons prepared mustard
350 g/12 oz streaky bacon
100 ml/4 fl oz olive oil
lettuce leaves
lemon slices
sprigs parsley

Sprinkle the herrings with the lemon juice and season lightly with salt. Open out the filleted herrings, spread the mustard over the insides and close them up again. Wrap the bacon rashers round them. Heat the oil in a pan and fry the herrings for about 10 minutes each side, until crisp. Arrange on top of the lettuce leaves, and garnish with the lemon slices and parsley. Serve at once, with a potato salad.

Trout with Capers

juice 1 lemon
4 trout (250 g/9 oz each), cleaned
salt
flour for coating
100 ml/4 fl oz oil
75 g/3 oz butter
100 g/4 oz breadcrumbs
1 small bottle capers, drained
lemon slices
sprigs parsley

Pour half the lemon juice over the trout and leave to stand for 5 minutes. Season with salt inside and out, and coat with flour. Heat the oil in a pan and fry the trout for 5 minutes each side, until golden brown. Remove from the pan and pour off the oil. Melt the butter in the pan and fry the trout for another 5 minutes each side. Remove and arrange on a warmed dish. Put the breadcrumbs in the pan and fry until light brown. Sprinkle them over the trout, pour on the remaining lemon juice, and scatter the capers on top. Garnish with the lemon slices and parsley, and serve at once.

Windsor herrings

Right: trout with capers

Mackerel with soured cream

Mackerel with Soured Cream

juice 1 lemon
4 mackerel (200 g/7 oz each),
  cleaned
25 g/1 oz butter
2 onions, chopped

100 g/4 oz tomatoes, skinned,
  seeded and chopped
salt, pepper, dried thyme
100 g/4 oz mushrooms, sliced
4 tablespoons soured cream,
  whipped

Pour the lemon juice over the mackerel, cover and leave to stand for 10 minutes. Melt the butter in a large frying pan and fry the onions until yellow. Add the tomatoes, stir well, and season with salt, pepper and thyme. Add the mushrooms and fry gently for 10 minutes. Place the mackerel on top of the vegetable mixture, cover and continue cooking gently over low heat for 20 minutes. Arrange on a warmed dish, pour the cream over the mackerel and serve.

Grilled Cod and Bacon

4 cod fillets (250 g/9 oz each)
4 tablespoons oil
salt, pepper
225 g/8 oz streaky bacon

30 g/1¼ oz butter
½ lemon, cut into wedges
sprigs parsley

Paint the cod fillets with oil and season them. Place on the rack of the grill, with the grill pan underneath to catch the drips, and grill for 8 minutes each side. Meanwhile, cut the bacon rashers in half and fry them in a frying pan until crisp. Melt the butter in a small saucepan.

Arrange the cod fillets and bacon on warmed plates, and pour the butter over the fish. Serve, garnished with the lemon wedges and parsley. Boiled new potatoes, tossed in butter and sprinkled with chopped parsley, go well with this dish.

Baked Cod with Lemon
(see overleaf)

750 g/1½ lb fillet of cod
2 lemons
3 onions, chopped
150 ml/¼ pint white wine
60 g/2½ oz breadcrumbs

40 g/1½ oz butter, cut into pieces
1 teaspoon chopped parsley
1 teaspoon chopped dill
salt, pepper

Cut the cod into 5 cm/2 inch pieces. Grease a casserole with butter and put in the pieces of cod. Peel the lemons and cut them into thin slices, removing any pips. Use to cover the fish. Arrange the onions over the lemon slices and pour on the wine. Sprinkle the breadcrumbs on top and dab with the butter pieces. Lastly, sprinkle on the parsley and dill and season. Place on the bottom shelf of the oven and bake at 220°C/425°F/gas 7 for 25 minutes. Remove from the oven and serve immediately.

Grilled cod and bacon

Baked cod with lemon

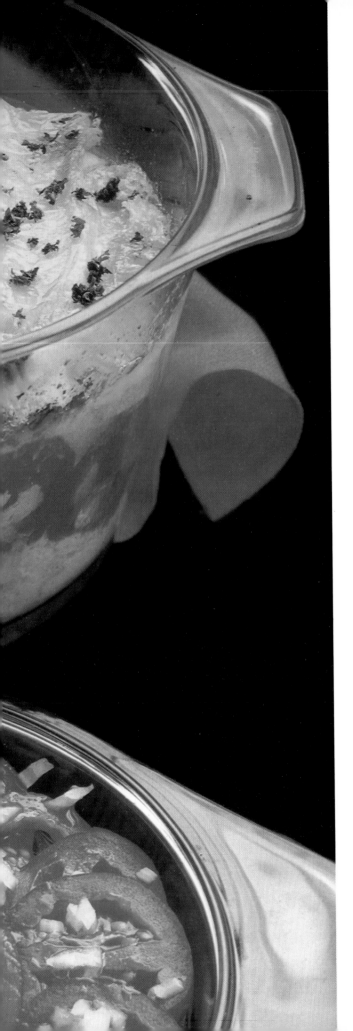

Fish and Cheese Casserole

juice 1 lemon
450 g/1 lb fillet of cod
salt, pepper, mild paprika
250 g/9 oz tomatoes, skinned,
  seeded and quartered

250 g/9 oz Camembert cheese,
  thinly sliced
150 ml/¼ pint single cream
1 tablespoon chopped parsley

Sprinkle the lemon juice over the cod and season with plenty of paprika. Grease a casserole with butter. Put in half the cod and season with salt and paprika. Put the tomatoes on top, season with salt, then add the rest of the cod. Season again with salt and paprika. Cover with the cheese slices. Season the cream lightly with salt and pepper and pour over the dish. Sprinkle the parsley on top. Bake at 200°C/400°F/gas 6 for 30 minutes. Remove from the oven and serve immediately with a tomato and onion salad.

Cod in White Wine Sauce

2 kg/4 lb mussels
250 ml/8 fl oz water
250 ml/8 fl oz white wine
1 bay leaf
4 juniper berries
2 peppercorns
rind ½ lemon
salt

sugar
150 g/5 oz peeled prawns or
  shrimps
4 cod steaks (250 g/9 oz each)
juice 1 lemon
1 egg yolk
150 ml/¼ pint single cream
1 teaspoon chopped dill

Scrub the mussels thoroughly under cold water. Boil up the water and wine in a large pan, and add the bay leaf, juniper berries, peppercorns and lemon rind. Season with salt and sugar. When the liquid is boiling hard, add the mussels, cover the pan and cook for 5 minutes. Then remove the mussels from the liquid, take them out of their shells and remove the beards. Keep the mussels warm in a covered dish in the oven.

Add the prawns or shrimps to the pan and heat gently for 5 minutes. Remove, drain and add to the shelled mussels. Keep hot.

Season the cod steaks with the lemon juice and leave to stand for 5 minutes. Reheat the liquid in the pan until nearly boiling, put in the fish steaks and let them poach for 10 minutes, until cooked. Remove and drain. Put them on a warmed dish and keep hot.

To make the sauce, pour the liquid through a sieve into another pan. Boil until reduced by half, and then remove from the heat. Whisk the egg yolk and cream together and add to the liquid. Stir in the dill. Arrange the mussels and prawns or shrimps round the cod steaks, pour the sauce over and serve.

Fish and cheese casserole

Cod pie

Cod Pie

600 g/1¼ lb potatoes
2 tablespoons white wine
  vinegar
1 bay leaf
4 black peppercorns
1 kg/2 lb fillet of cod
75 g/3 oz butter
1 onion, chopped
40 g/1½ oz cooked ham, chopped

40 g/1½ oz flour
250 ml/8 fl oz stock
350 ml/12 fl oz milk
salt, pepper, grated nutmeg
1 egg yolk
50 g/2 oz Parmesan cheese,
  grated
2 tomatoes, skinned and
  quartered

Bring a pan of salted water to the boil, add the potatoes and simmer for 20 minutes, until done. Meanwhile, bring another pan of water to the boil, and add the vinegar, bay leaf and peppercorns. Then add the fish and poach over gentle heat for 7 minutes, until done.

To make the sauce, melt half the butter in a pan. Add the onion and ham and fry until pale yellow. Stir in the flour and fry gently for 3 minutes. Add the stock and 250 ml/8 fl oz of the milk. Bring to the boil, stirring all the time, and simmer for 10 minutes. Season with salt and pepper.

Drain the potatoes and sieve them into a bowl. Bring the remaining milk to near boiling point in a pan, and pour over the potato. Mix in with a whisk. Stir in the egg yolk and season with salt and nutmeg.

Grease a casserole with butter and line the base and sides with the potato purée. Put 100 ml/4 fl oz of sauce into the casserole. Drain the fish, skin and bone it, and flake the flesh. Add to the casserole. Pour the remaining sauce over, sprinkle the cheese on top, and dab with the remaining butter, cut into flakes. Place on the bottom shelf of the oven and bake at 240°C/475°F/gas 9 for 15 minutes. Remove from the oven and serve immediately, garnished with the tomatoes.

Meat

Meat

Fillet of Beef in Puff Pastry

SERVES 6

salt, pepper, paprika
750 g/1½ lb fillet of beef,
  in one piece
2 tablespoons oil
1 white bread roll, crusts
  removed
150 ml/¼ pint milk
350 g/12 oz lean veal

20 g/¾ oz butter
1 small onion, chopped
1 tablespoon chopped parsley
2 eggs, beaten
2 tablespoons single cream
450 g/1 lb puff pastry
1 egg, separated

Rub salt and pepper into the beef fillet. Heat the oil in a roasting pan and brown the fillet, at a high temperature, for 3 minutes each side. Reduce the heat and fry for another 5 minutes each side. Allow to cool.

To make the stuffing, break the bread roll into pieces and soak in the milk for 15 minutes. Put the veal through the mincer and place in a bowl. Squeeze out the bread and crumble it. Melt the butter in a pan, add the bread, onion and parsley, and fry for 5 minutes, stirring. Mix with the veal. Stir in the beaten eggs and the cream. Season generously with salt, pepper and paprika, and mix thoroughly.

Roll out the pastry on a lightly floured surface into a rectangle large enough to wrap round the fillet, with extra space for the stuffing. (Leave a little pastry aside for decoration.) Paint the edges of the pastry with the egg white. Place just over half the stuffing down the middle of the pastry; the area covered should be larger than the fillet. Place the fillet on the stuffing, and spread the remaining stuffing on top. Join the edges of the pastry on top and at the ends of the fillet, pressing together firmly. Turn the parcel over so that the joined edges are underneath, and place on a greased baking sheet.

Cut out decorative shapes from the remaining pastry and use to decorate the top of the pastry case. Beat the egg yolk and use to glaze the top and sides of the pastry case. Bake at 200°C/400°F/gas 6 for 45 minutes. Remove from the oven and allow to rest for 5 minutes. Carve into slices and serve.

Steak and Kidney Pie

250 g/9 oz kidney
20 g/¾ oz butter
2 onions, chopped
1 tablespoon chopped parsley
salt, pepper
25 g/1 oz cornflour

300 g/10 oz top rump of beef,
  cut into cubes
150 g/5 oz mushrooms, sliced
250 ml/8 fl oz hot stock
150 g/5 oz puff pastry
1 egg yolk, beaten

Cut out the core from the kidney, and slice the kidney. Melt the butter in a pan and fry the onions until they begin to soften. Add the parsley and remove the pan from the heat. Generously season the cornflour and toss the meat and kidney in it.

Put the meat and kidney, mushrooms, and the onion and parsley mixture into a pie dish or shallow ovenproof dish. Pour in the stock. Roll out the pastry on a lightly floured surface and use to cover the pie, knocking up the edges. Make a hole in the centre to allow steam to escape. Roll out any scraps of pastry and use to decorate the pie. Glaze the pie crust with the egg yolk. Bake at 200°C/400°/gas 6 for 1 hour. Cover the pie with greaseproof paper if the crust begins to over-brown during cooking. Remove from the oven when cooked and serve immediately.

Fillet of beef in puff pastry

Stuffed Pot Roast of Beef

750 g/1½ lb sirloin of beef, cut
   fairly flat
salt, pepper, grated nutmeg
½ teaspoon prepared mustard
30 g/1¼ oz butter
4 onions, chopped
40 g/1½ oz breadcrumbs
2 tablespoons chopped parsley
1 egg, beaten
50 g/2 oz lard
100 g/4 oz lean bacon, chopped
1 teaspoon dried chervil
½ teaspoon dried tarragon
250 ml/8 fl oz red wine
100 ml/4 fl oz hot stock

Trim off any fat from the meat. Make a slit through the middle, leaving about 3 cm/1 inch at the end not cut through. Season inside and out with salt and pepper. Paint the inside thinly with mustard. Roll up the meat (now a large flat slice) in aluminium foil, and set aside.

To make the stuffing, melt the butter in a pan. Fry half the onions for 3 minutes. Sprinkle in the breadcrumbs and fry for another 5 minutes, stirring. Transfer the onion and breadcrumb mixture to a bowl and mix in 1 tablespoon of the parsley, and the egg. Season with salt, pepper and nutmeg. Unroll the meat and spread it with the stuffing. Roll up again firmly, and fasten with string or cocktail sticks.

Melt the lard in a large flameproof casserole, and brown the joint well on all sides for 10 minutes. Add the bacon and remaining onions to the pan after 7 minutes. Sprinkle the remaining parsley, the chervil and the tarragon over the meat. Pour in the wine and stock, cover tightly, and braise the joint over low heat for about 1½ hours. Remove the meat from the pan, cover it, and let it stand for 5 to 10 minutes. Then carve it into slices and keep hot on a warmed dish. Strain the meat juices, pour a little over the meat, and hand the rest separately in a sauceboat. Serve at once.

Savoury Cheese Mince

40 g/1½ oz butter
1 large onion, chopped
250 g/9 oz minced beef
250 g/9 oz minced pork
salt, pepper
250 g/9 oz canned tomatoes
200 g/7 oz spaghetti
350 ml/12 fl oz stock
250 g/9 oz frozen peas
150 ml/¼ pint red wine
2 large slices Gouda cheese
sprig parsley

Melt the butter in a flameproof casserole and fry the onion until it begins to soften. Add the minced meats and fry, stirring all the time, until well browned. Season with salt and pepper. Reserve 3 tomatoes for the topping; add the rest to the meat, with their liquid. Break the spaghetti into pieces about 7 cm/2¾ inches long and add to the casserole. Pour in the stock. Bring to the boil, cover, and simmer for 10 minutes until all the ingredients are just tender. Add the peas and continue to simmer until thawed. Stir in the wine. Arrange the slices of cheese over the meat, and place the reserved tomatoes on top. Bake at 240°C/475°F/gas 9, on the bottom of the oven, for 10 to 15 minutes. Remove from the oven and serve garnished with the parsley.

Savoury cheese mince

Stuffed pot roast of beef

Salt beef

Salt Beef

750 g/1½ lb salt brisket of beef
1 large onion
1 leek
1 bay leaf
5 peppercorns
5 allspice berries

1 tablespoon chopped parsley
100 g/4 oz horseradish root,
  grated
80 ml/3 fl oz single cream
sprig parsley

Soak the meat in cold water for 1 hour before use. Drain and put in a large saucepan. Add the onion, leek, bay leaf, peppercorns, allspice berries and plenty of water. Bring to the boil, skim off any froth or bits that rise to the surface, and simmer for 1½ hours.

Meanwhile mix together the chopped parsley, horseradish and cream. Place in a small bowl and garnish with the sprig of parsley. Remove the beef from the pan when cooked, carve into slices, and arrange on a warmed plate. Pour a little of the cooking liquid over the meat, and serve at once with the horseradish sauce.

Beef casserole

Beef Casserole

750 g/1½ lb top rump of beef
salt, pepper, paprika
2 tablespoons oil
30 g/1¼ oz butter
150 g/5 oz streaky bacon,
  chopped

250 g/9 oz onions, sliced
600 g/1¼ lb potatoes, thinly sliced
3 small pickled cucumbers,
  sliced
250 ml/8 fl oz hot stock
1 bay leaf

Cut the meat into slices 1 cm/½ inch thick, and season with pepper and paprika. Heat the oil in a pan, and brown the meat slices for 1 minute each side. Remove and set aside. Melt the butter in another pan, add the bacon, and fry for 5 minutes. Add the onions and fry for a further 5 minutes, until golden yellow.

Arrange the meat, bacon and onions, potatoes and cucumbers in layers in an ovenproof casserole, seasoning each layer with a little salt and pepper. Pour in the stock, place the bay leaf on top, cover with a lid and cook at 200°C/400°F/gas 6 for 1 hour. Remove the bay leaf and serve straight from the casserole.

Beef goulash

Beef Goulash

50 g/2 oz lard
750 g/1½ lb braising steak, cut into cubes
350 g/12 oz onions, sliced
2 tablespoons mild paprika
1 teaspoon ground cumin
1 teaspoon dried marjoram

salt, pepper, garlic salt
100 ml/4 fl oz hot water
2 tablespoons vinegar
30 g/1¼ oz flour
150 ml/¼ pint hot stock
250 ml/8 fl oz soured cream

Melt the lard in a flameproof casserole and brown the meat on all sides for 5 minutes. Add the onions and season with the paprika, cumin, marjoram and a pinch of garlic salt. Stir well and fry for 5 minutes. Then add the water and vinegar, cover the casserole, and let the meat braise gently for 1½ hours.

Mix the flour to a smooth paste in a cup with a little cold water. Blend a little of the hot liquid into the mixture, then return to the pan. Stir in the hot stock. Bring slowly to the boil, stirring constantly. Simmer for 8 minutes. Season with salt and pepper. Pour the cream into the middle and stir it in when the dish is brought to the table for serving.

Oxtail Casserole

1·25 kg/2¾ lb oxtail
75 g/3 oz beef dripping
1 onion, quartered
1 stick celery, chopped
1 leek, chopped
600 g/1¼ lb carrots, sliced

1·5 litres/2½ pints water
salt, pepper, dried marjoram
1 kg/2 lb potatoes
1 tablespoon chopped parsley
150 ml/¼ pint soured cream

Cut the oxtail into pieces 3 cm/1¼ inches long, and trim off as much fat as possible. Heat the dripping in a casserole, and brown the oxtail pieces on all sides for 10 minutes. Add the onion, celery, leek and 1 sliced carrot, and fry for another 5 minutes. Pour in the water and season with salt. Bring to the boil and simmer, tightly covered, for 2 hours.

Cut the potatoes into large cubes. Take the pieces of oxtail out of the stock and set aside. Strain the stock and return to the casserole. Add the potatoes and the rest of the carrots, and simmer for 20 minutes, or until tender. Meanwhile, remove the meat from the bones and cut it into small pieces. Add to the vegetables. Season with salt, pepper and marjoram, and reheat to just below boiling point. Remove from the heat and stir in the parsley and cream. Serve immediately.

Gammon with Green Beans

60 g/2¼ oz streaky bacon
2 onions, chopped
600 g/1¼ lb lean gammon, cut into cubes
lard as required
1.5 litres/2½ pints stock
600 g/1¼ lb French beans, topped, tailed and cut into even lengths
350 g/12 oz potatoes, sliced
2 leeks, sliced
2 sprigs savory
salt, pepper
sprigs parsley

Fry the bacon gently in a pan until the fat runs. Add the onions and fry for a few minutes. Add the gammon and brown on all sides. Add a little lard if necessary. Pour the stock into the pan, bring to the boil and simmer for 1 hour.

Add the beans, potatoes, leeks and savory to the pan, and season to taste. Simmer for about 30 minutes longer, or until the vegetables are cooked. Serve, garnished with the parsley.

Pork Chops Baked with Apples *(see overleaf)*

4 pork chops (150 g/5 oz each)
salt, pepper, fennel seeds
75 g/3 oz butter
450 g/1 lb dessert apples, peeled, cored and sliced
sprig rosemary

Season the chops with salt, pepper and fennel. Melt half the butter in a frying pan, and brown the chops for 3 minutes each side. Arrange half the apples over the base of the casserole. Place the chops and the fat from the pan on top, and arrange the remaining apples round the chops. Divide the rest of the butter into small pieces and scatter on top of the apples. Lay the sprig of rosemary on top of the chops and cover the casserole. Bake at 200°C/400°F/gas 6 for 20 minutes. Take out of the oven and serve from the casserole.

Gammon with green beans

Overleaf: pork chops baked with apples

Stuffed belly of pork

Stuffed Belly of Pork

SERVES 6

1 kg/2 lb lean, boned belly of
  pork, with the rind on
40 g/1½ oz butter
3 small onions, chopped
1 cooking apple, peeled, cored
  and chopped
250 g/9 oz pig's or calf's liver
1 tablespoon chopped parsley
30 g/1¼ oz breadcrumbs

1 teaspoon dried marjoram
salt, pepper
½ onion
½ teaspoon ground cumin
60 g/2½ oz lard
500 ml/18 fl oz hot water
1 tablespoon cornflour
3 tablespoons Madeira

Make a slit in the side of the joint to take the stuffing. To
make the stuffing, melt the butter in a pan and fry the small
onions for 3 minutes. Add the apple and fry for another 2
minutes. Remove the onion and apple and put into a bowl,
leaving as much fat as possible behind in the pan. Remove
any membrane or tubes from the liver. Chop the liver finely
and fry for 2 minutes in the fat left in the pan. Add to the
bowl. Sprinkle the parsley, breadcrumbs and marjoram into
the bowl and mix together to make a stuffing. Season well.

Stuff the pork with this mixture and sew up the slit. Rub the
meat well with the cut surface of the half onion. Season the
cumin with salt and pepper, and rub this mixture into the
meat. Make crossways cuts in the rind to form a diamond
pattern. Heat the lard in a large pan and brown the joint on
all sides for 10 minutes. Pour in 250 ml/8 fl oz of the water.
Cover the meat and braise for 1 hour over gentle heat.
If necessary, add a little more water during the cooking
time to prevent drying out.

Remove the joint from the pan and keep hot. Stir up the
juices left in the pan, stirring in the remaining water. Pour off
any fat if necessary. Mix the cornflour to a smooth paste with
a little cold water in a cup. Blend a little of the hot sauce into
the mixture, then return to the pan. Bring slowly to the boil,
stirring constantly. Simmer for 2 to 3 minutes. Season to taste
with salt, pepper and the Madeira. Strain the sauce into a
warmed sauceboat and keep hot.

Remove the thread from the meat. Cut the meat into slices
for serving and hand the sauce separately.

Roast ham

Roast Ham

2 teaspoons prepared mustard
1 teaspoon dried thyme
salt, pepper, paprika
750 g/1½ lb lean joint of gammon
1 stick celery, chopped
1 carrot, chopped
1 leek, chopped

250 ml/8 fl oz boiling water
30 g/1¼ oz butter
30 g/1¼ oz flour
150 ml/¼ pint red wine
2 tablespoons soured cream
sprig parsley

Mix together the mustard and thyme to make a paste. Season with salt and pepper. Rub this mixture into the joint. Put the celery, carrot and leek into a large roasting pan, and pour the water over them. Place the joint of gammon on top. Bake at 220°C/425°F/gas 7 for 1½ hours, basting the joint from time to time with the pan juices.

Remove the joint from the oven, place in a warmed dish, cover and keep hot. Stir up all the juices and residues in the roasting pan and strain through a sieve. To make the sauce, melt the butter in a pan, add the flour, and fry for 3 minutes over gentle heat, stirring, until brown. Slowly stir in the strained pan juices and the wine. Simmer for 5 minutes. Season with salt, pepper and paprika. Remove the pan from the heat and stir in the cream. Reheat gently without boiling. Pour the sauce into a warmed sauceboat and keep hot. To serve, carve the ham into slices and garnish with the parsley. Hand the sauce separately.

Pork Hot-pot *(see overleaf)*

50 g/2 oz lard
750 g/1½ lb shoulder of pork, cut into cubes
375 g/13 oz onions, sliced
375 g/13 oz green peppers, seeded and chopped

60 g/2½ oz canned tomato purée
250 ml/8 fl oz hot stock
salt, pepper
2 tablespoons mild paprika
150 ml/¼ pint single cream

Melt the lard in a pan and brown the meat on all sides for 5 minutes. Add the onion and fry for another 5 minutes. Then add the peppers. Mix together the tomato purée and stock, and pour into the pan. Season with salt, pepper and the paprika. Cover the pan and simmer gently for 1 hour. Stir in the cream, transfer to a warmed dish and serve immediately.

Overleaf: pork hot-pot

Ham and cheese roll

Ham soufflé

Ham and Cheese Roll

SERVES 6

300 g/10 oz puff pastry
300 g/10 oz cooked ham, thinly
   sliced
300 g/10 oz Gouda cheese, thinly
   sliced
200 g/7 oz dessert apples, peeled,
   cored and sliced

50 g/2 oz sliced salami
6 tomatoes, sliced
1 tablespoon chopped chives
dried oregano
1 egg yolk, beaten

Roll out the pastry on a lightly floured surface to a rectangle 45 × 36 cm/18 × 14 inches. Cut a 3 cm/1¼ inch strip off the edge for decoration. Cover the middle third of the pastry rectangle with half the ham. Cut the cheese slices into strips, and arrange on the ham alternately with the apple. Place the salami on top, and the tomatoes on top of the salami. (Skin the tomatoes first if you prefer.) Sprinkle the chives and a small pinch oregano over the ingredients, and cover with the remaining ham.

   Paint the edges of the pastry with cold water. Fold the long sides of the rectangle up over the ingredients, making sure both ends are folded in and well sealed. Cut out decorative

shapes from the reserved strip of pastry and use to garnish the top of the roll. Glaze with the beaten egg yolk. Bake at 220°C/425°F/gas 7 for 30 minutes. Remove from the oven and cut into slices for serving.

Ham Soufflé

90 g/3½ oz butter
2 onions, chopped
450 g/1 lb cooked ham, chopped
6 eggs, separated

150 ml/¼ pint single cream
1 tablespoon chopped parsley
1 tablespoon chopped chives
salt, grated nutmeg, cayenne

Melt 60 g/2½ oz of butter in a pan and fry the onions for 3 minutes until golden yellow. Remove the pan from the heat and mix in the ham. Generously grease a large soufflé dish and put in the ham and onion mixture. Beat together the egg yolks, cream, parsley and chives. Season well with salt, nutmeg and cayenne. Separately, beat the egg whites until stiff and fold carefully into the egg yolk mixture. Place this mixture on top of the ham and onions. Cut the remaining butter into flakes and scatter on top. Bake at 220°C/425°F/gas 7 for 25 minutes. Remove from the oven and serve at once.

Boiled leg of mutton with caper sauce

Boiled Leg of Mutton with Caper Sauce

1 kg/2 lb boned leg of mutton
2 onions
juice 2 lemons
150 ml/¼ pint wine vinegar
1·7 litres/3 pints water
2 cloves garlic
salt, pepper
2 bay leaves
4 cloves

2 tablespoons chopped parsley
2 teaspoons chopped dill
1 stick celery, chopped
1 carrot, chopped
1 leek, chopped
40 g/1½ oz butter
40 g/1½ oz flour
150 ml/¼ pint soured cream
small bottle capers

Remove any skin from the meat. To make the marinade, grate 1 of the onions finely. Press the onion juice into a large shallow bowl through a linen cloth. Stir in half the lemon juice, the vinegar and 250 ml/8 fl oz of the water. Crush the garlic cloves with plenty of salt and crumble 1 of the bay leaves. Add to the marinade with the cloves, 1 tablespoon of the parsley and the dill. Stir thoroughly. Put the meat into the marinade, cover and leave to stand for 24 hours, turning from time to time.

Bring the remaining water to the boil in a large pan and add salt. Take the meat out of the marinade, pat dry, and add to the pan. Simmer for 20 minutes. Cut the second onion into quarters and add to the pan with the celery, carrot, leek and remaining bay leaf. Simmer for another 40 minutes. Remove the meat from the pan and keep hot. Strain the stock.

To make the sauce, melt the butter in a pan, add the flour and fry gently. Stir in 250 ml/8 fl oz of the hot stock, bring to the boil and simmer for 8 minutes. Remove the pan from the heat, stir in the cream and remaining lemon juice, and season to taste with salt and pepper. Finally, add the capers with their liquid. Reheat gently without boiling.

To serve, cut the mutton into thick slices and arrange on a warmed dish. Pour the caper sauce over it and sprinkle with the remaining parsley.

Lamb and vegetable casserole

Lamb and Vegetable Casserole

4 tablespoons oil
450 g/1 lb boned shoulder of
  lamb, cut into cubes
1 onion, chopped
400 g/14 oz savoy cabbage,
  shredded
250 g/9 oz celeriac root, diced
250 g/9 oz carrots, sliced
1 leek, sliced
1.5 litres/2½ pints hot stock

250 g/9 oz potatoes, diced
250 g/9 oz French beans, topped,
  tailed and cut into even lengths
1 small cauliflower, divided into
  florets
2 tablespoons tomato purée
salt, pepper
1 tablespoon chopped parsley

Heat the oil in a pan and brown the meat on all sides. Add the onion and fry until golden. Transfer the meat and onion to a flameproof casserole, add the cabbage, celeriac, carrots and leek, and pour on the stock. Bring to the boil and simmer for 1¼ hours. Add the potatoes, beans and cauliflower 20 minutes before the end of the cooking time.

Mix the tomato purée with a little of the cooking liquid, then stir back into the casserole. Season to taste. Sprinkle the parsley over the casserole and serve.

Lamb pilau

Lamb Pilau

50 g/2 oz butter
450 g/1 lb boned shoulder of
 lamb, cut into cubes
4 onions, chopped
salt, pepper
750 ml/1¼ pints hot water

200 g/7 oz long-grain rice
250 g/9 oz tomatoes, skinned,
 seeded and chopped
mild paprika
sugar

Melt the butter in a pan and brown the meat on all sides for 5 minutes. Add the onions and fry for another 5 minutes. Season with salt and pepper. Pour in the water, bring to the boil, cover, and simmer over medium heat for 1 hour. Add the rice to the pan after 40 minutes, and add the tomatoes 5 minutes before the end of the cooking time. Add a little more water during cooking if necessary. Take 1 tablespoon of the hot liquid from the pan, stir in a pinch of paprika and sugar, and return to the pan. Stir, adjust seasoning if necessary, and serve, with a green pepper and onion salad.

Crown of lamb

Crown of Lamb

2 kg/4 lb saddle of lamb
salt, pepper, garlic salt, dried sage
600 ml/1 pint hot stock
150 ml/¼ pint white wine
300 g/10 oz French beans, topped,
  tailed and cut into even lengths

20 g/¾ oz butter
1 onion, chopped
1 tablespoon flour
75 g/3 oz yogurt
3 tomatoes, halved

Get the butcher to saw through the saddle of lamb down the backbone. Have the backbone removed. Trim the layer of fat from the back and chop down between the rib bones. Bend both halves of the saddle round into a semicircle, and tie them together with string to form a crown. Rub in salt, pepper and garlic salt. Put the crown of lamb in a roasting pan and pour in 350 ml/12 fl oz of the stock, and the wine. Cover with foil and roast at 180°C/350°F/gas 4 for 2 hours. Remove the foil after 1 hour.

About 25 minutes before the meat has finished cooking, bring a pan of salted water to the boil. Add the beans and simmer for 15 minutes, or until tender. Drain in a sieve. Melt the butter in a pan and fry the onion for 5 minutes, until golden. Add the beans and a pinch of sage. Remove from the heat, cover and keep hot. Take the meat out of the oven, remove the string, and put the crown of lamb on a warmed serving dish. Keep hot.

To make the gravy, add the remaining stock to the juices in the roasting pan and stir. Mix the flour to a smooth paste in a cup with a little cold water. Blend a little of the hot liquid into the mixture, then return to the pan. Bring slowly to the boil, stirring constantly. Simmer for 5 minutes. Stir in the yogurt and season. Transfer to a sauceboat and keep hot.

To serve, place the onion and beans in the centre and around the meat. Garnish with tomatoes. Hand the gravy separately.

Ragout of Mutton

750 g/1½ lb boned shoulder of
  mutton or lamb, cut into cubes
salt
4 tablespoons oil
1 onion, chopped
1 clove garlic, chopped
powdered saffron
1 tablespoon flour
150 ml/¼ pint white wine

250 ml/8 fl oz stock
195 g/6¾ oz jar pearl onions,
  drained
200 g/7 oz carrots, chopped
200 g/7 oz celeriac root, chopped
150 ml/¼ pint single cream
1 tablespoon cornflour
1 teaspoon chopped chives

Sprinkle the meat with salt. Heat the oil in a large pan and fry the meat, onion and garlic for 7 minutes. Add a pinch of saffron. Sprinkle on the flour and stir in the wine and stock. Cover the pan and simmer for 10 minutes. Add the pearl onions, carrots and celeriac to the meat. Bring back to the boil and continue to simmer for another 50 minutes, over low heat. Mix the cream and cornflour together in a cup. Stir into the ragout over gentle heat. Serve, garnished with the chives.

Rolled Roast Veal

1 kg/2 lb boned shoulder or
  breast of veal
salt, pepper, dried sage, dried
  rosemary
1 tablespoon prepared mustard
1 tablespoon lemon juice
200 g/7 oz minced beef
1 onion, finely chopped
175 g/6 oz canned mushrooms,
  drained and chopped

1 tablespoon chopped parsley
1½ leeks
1 egg yolk
Tabasco sauce
4 tablespoons oil
1 stick celery, chopped
1 carrot, chopped
150 ml/¼ pint brown ale
250 ml/8 fl oz hot stock
2 teaspoons cornflour

Season the veal with salt and pepper. Mix together the
mustard and lemon juice, and paint over the inside of the
veal. To make the stuffing, put the minced beef in a bowl.
Add the onion, mushrooms and parsley. Finely chop the half
leek and add to the bowl. Then add the egg yolk, and season
with salt, pepper, Tabasco sauce and the herbs. Mix well.

Spread the stuffing over the inside of the veal. Roll the meat
up and fasten with thread. Heat the oil in a roasting pan, put
the rolled veal into the pan, and roast on the bottom shelf of
the oven, at 200°C/400°F/gas 6, for 1½ hours.

Chop the whole leek and add to the meat, with the celery
and carrot, after 15 minutes. Paint or baste the joint from
time to time with the brown ale.

Remove the pan from the oven and keep the meat hot on a
warmed dish. Strain the pan juices through a sieve, and add
the stock. Return the liquid to the pan and heat gently. Mix
the cornflour to a smooth paste in a cup with a little cold
water. Blend a little of the hot liquid into the mixture, then
return to the pan. Bring slowly to the boil, stirring constantly.
Simmer for 2 to 3 minutes. Season the gravy and pour into a
warmed sauceboat. Serve the meat and gravy separately.

Rolled roast veal

Stuffed Veal

SERVES 8

75 g/3 oz smoked streaky bacon, finely chopped
1 onion, finely chopped
125 g/4½ oz canned chanterelle mushrooms, drained and finely chopped
1 teaspoon chopped parsley
1 teaspoon chopped dill
1 teaspoon dried tarragon
1 teaspoon dried basil

200 g/7 oz minced beef
75 g/3 oz breadcrumbs
3 eggs
225 ml/7 fl oz soured cream
salt, pepper
1.5 kg/3 lb boned breast of veal
4 tablespoons oil
500 ml/18 fl oz hot stock
20 g/¾ oz cornflour

To make the stuffing, fry the bacon in a pan until the fat runs. Add the onion and fry for 5 minutes. Then add the mushrooms and fry for another 5 minutes. Allow to cool, and then put into a bowl. Mix in the herbs, minced beef, breadcrumbs, eggs and 100 ml/4 fl oz of the soured cream. Season generously with salt and pepper. Using a sharp knife, cut a deep pouch in the veal, and fill this with the stuffing. Close the opening with cocktail sticks. Rub salt and pepper into the veal. Heat the oil in a roasting pan, but the breast of veal into it, and roast at 220°C/425°F/gas 7 for 1½ hours. Baste from time to time with a little of the hot stock.

Remove the pan from the oven and keep the meat hot on a warmed dish. Pour the remaining stock into the pan and stir up the pan juices. Pour this gravy into a saucepan and reheat. Mix together the cornflour and remaining cream. Stir into the gravy and bring to the boil, stirring continuously. Simmer for 2 to 3 minutes, season to taste, and pour into a warmed sauceboat. Serve the meat and gravy separately.

Veal Casserole

SERVES 6

100 g/4 oz streaky bacon, chopped
3 tablespoons oil
750 g/1½ lb lean veal, cut into cubes
salt, pepper, paprika
250 g/9 oz onions, chopped
2 cloves garlic, chopped
250 g/9 oz green peppers, seeded and chopped
500 ml/18 fl oz stock
250 g/9 oz carrots, sliced
450 g/1 lb tomatoes, skinned, seeded and quartered
250 g/9 oz long-grain rice
1 tablespoon chopped parsley

Heat the bacon in a pan until the fat runs. Add the oil and brown the veal on all sides for 10 minutes. Remove the bacon and veal from the pan, leaving behind as much fat as possible, season with salt and keep hot. Fry the onions, garlic and peppers quickly in the fat left in the pan. Remove from the pan and drain.

Heat the stock in a large pan, add the fried vegetables, the carrots and tomatoes, and simmer for 10 minutes. Season with salt, pepper and paprika. Then add the rice. Place the contents of the pan in a large casserole, and lay the veal and bacon on top. Seal the top of the casserole with aluminium foil as well as the lid, and cook at 200°C/400°F/gas 6 for 40 minutes. Remove from the oven, sprinkle on the parsley and serve immediately.

Blanquette of Veal

salt, pepper
750 g/1½ lb boned shoulder or neck of veal, cut into cubes
40 g/1½ oz margarine
3 onions, chopped
250 g/9 oz mushrooms, sliced
250 ml/8 fl oz hot stock
100 ml/4 fl oz white wine
1 tablespoon flour
150 ml/¼ pint single cream
1 teaspoon dried tarragon
1 tablespoon chopped chervil or parsley

Season the meat. Melt the margarine in a pan and brown the meat on all sides for 10 minutes. Add the onions and mushrooms, and fry gently for 5 minutes. Add the stock and wine, bring to the boil, cover and simmer for 45 minutes.

Mix together the flour, cream and tarragon in a small bowl. Remove the pan from the heat and stir in the cream mixture. Reheat gently, without boiling; stir until the blanquette thickens. Sprinkle on the chopped chervil or parsley and serve.

Veal casserole

Meat and Vegetable Stew

SERVES 6

200 g/7 oz braising steak
200 g/7 oz boned shoulder of pork
200 g/7 oz boned leg of lamb
50 g/2 oz beef marrow, sliced
3 onions, sliced
4 carrots, sliced
250 g/9 oz celeriac root, cut into cubes
350 g/12 oz potatoes, cut into cubes
2 leeks, sliced
600 g/1¼ lb white cabbage, shredded
salt, pepper
1 teaspoon ground cumin
1 teaspoon dried marjoram
500 ml/18 fl oz water
1 teaspoon chopped parsley

Cut the braising steak, pork and lamb into cubes. Line a large pan with the slices of beef marrow. Fill the pan with alternating layers of meat and vegetables, finishing with a layer of vegetables. Season each layer with salt, pepper, cumin and marjoram. Pour the water into the pan, bring to the boil, cover, and simmer for 1½ hours over gentle heat. Do not stir.

Put the stew into a warmed serving dish, sprinkle with the parsley and serve.

Mixed Fry *(see overleaf)*

4 lambs' kidneys
2 cloves garlic
salt, pepper
4 lamb cutlets (175 g/6 oz each)
4 tomatoes
4 pork chipolata sausages
2 tablespoons oil, or as required
1 onion, sliced
100 g/4 oz mushrooms
4 rashers streaky bacon
sprigs parsley

Cut the kidneys apart lengthways and remove the white core. Soak the kidneys for 20 minutes in a bowl of cold water, changing the water several times. Remove and drain. Crush the garlic with salt and rub into the kidneys and lamb cutlets. Then season with pepper. Cut out the hard parts near the stems of the tomatoes, and make crossways cuts in the tops. Season with salt. Prick the skins of the sausages with a fork.

Heat 2 tablespoons oil in a large frying pan until very hot. Brown the cutlets quickly on both sides, then reduce the heat and put in the sausages. Fry gently for about 5 minutes, turning from time to time to ensure even cooking. Then put in the kidneys. After another 2 minutes put in the onion and mushrooms, followed by the bacon and tomatoes 3 minutes later. Continue frying everything for a further 5 minutes. Add more oil at any stage of the frying if necessary. Season to taste and serve at once, garnished with the parsley.

Overleaf: mixed fry

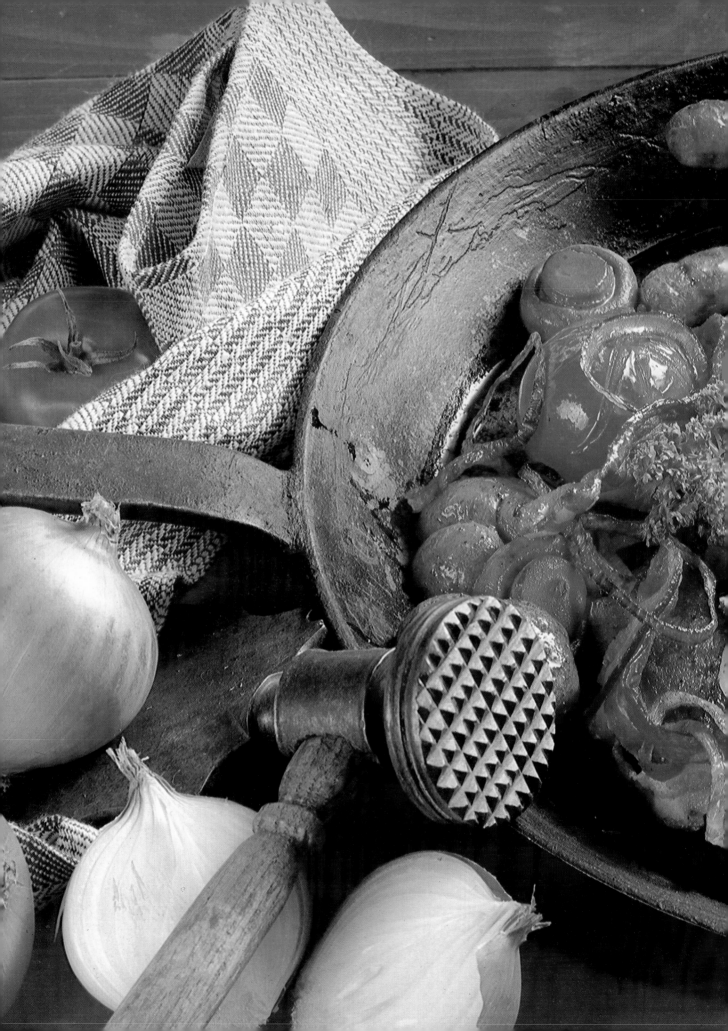

Meat loaf

Meat Loaf

SERVES 8

8 carrots
6 tomatoes
1 green pepper, seeded and
  chopped
450 g/1 lb minced beef
300 g/10 oz minced pork

1 onion, chopped
2 eggs, beaten
1 teaspoon mild paprika
2 teaspoons prepared mustard
salt, pepper
sprigs parsley

Bring a pan of salted water to the boil, and simmer the carrots for 15 minutes. Meanwhile prepare the meat mixture. Set aside 1 tomato for the garnish. Skin, seed and chop the rest. Mix together in a large bowl the pepper, chopped tomatoes, minced beef and pork, onion, eggs, paprika and mustard. Season, and knead the mixture well.

Line a rectangular loaf tin with oiled greaseproof paper. Half-fill with the meat mixture. Drain the carrots and arrange on top, then add the rest of the meat mixture. Press down well. Bake at 200°C/400°F/gas 6 for 1 hour.

Remove from the oven and allow to cool for about 10 minutes. Then carefully pour off the fat. Turn out the meat loaf on to an oval platter or dish. Garnish with the parsley, and with the remaining tomato, cut into wedges, and serve.

Poultry
and Game

Chicken Pie

PASTRY
250 g/9 oz butter
250 g/9 oz flour
salt
100 ml/4 fl oz iced water

FILLING
1 kg/2 lb boiling chicken
20 g/¾ oz butter
1 onion, chopped
20 g/¾ oz flour
250 ml/8 fl oz red wine
50 g/2 oz cooked ham, chopped
50 g/2 oz cooked ox tongue, chopped
salt, pepper
juice ½ lemon
20 g/¾ oz chopped almonds
20 g/¾ oz chopped pistachio nuts
3 black truffles, chopped
1 egg yolk, lightly beaten

To make the pastry, divide the butter in half. Place 1 portion in the refrigerator to chill. Melt the second portion and allow to cool. Sift the flour and a pinch of salt into a bowl. Divide the chilled butter into flakes and place on top of the flour. Rub in with the fingertips, working fast to keep the pastry cool. Stir in the melted, cooled butter and the water. Form into a ball and leave overnight in the refrigerator.

To make the filling, bring a large pan of salted water to the boil. Add the chicken and simmer for 1 hour, or until tender. Then take the chicken out of the pan, remove the skin and bones, and chop the meat. Melt the butter in another pan, and fry the onion gently until it begins to soften. Sprinkle on the flour and fry for 1 minute, stirring. Stir in the wine and bring to the boil. Add the chicken, ham and tongue, and simmer for 7 minutes. Season with salt, pepper and the lemon juice. Add the almonds, pistachio nuts and truffles. Mix thoroughly and allow to cool.

Grease a large pie dish with butter. Roll out two-thirds of the pastry on a lightly floured surface and use to line the pie dish. Place the filling in the dish. Roll out the remaining pastry to make the lid, cover the pie, and press the edges well together. Make a small hole in the centre to let out the steam. Cut out decorative shapes from any pastry scraps and use to decorate the pie. Glaze with the beaten egg yolk. Bake at 220°C/425°F/gas 7 for 35 minutes. Remove from the oven and serve immediately.

Chicken pie

Chicken pasties

Chicken Pasties

SERVES 6

600 g/1¼ lb cold roast chicken
1 tablespoon chopped parsley
4 tablespoons double cream, lightly whipped
salt, pepper

300 g/10 oz puff pastry
6 slices cooked ham
1 egg yolk, lightly beaten
6 teaspoons single cream

Remove the chicken meat from the bones. Chop it roughly and place in a bowl. Add the parsley and whipped cream, season well, and mix thoroughly.

Roll out the pastry on a lightly floured surface. Cut it into 6 squares 12 × 12 cm/4¾ × 4¾ inches large. Fold each slice of ham into 4, and place 1 on each pastry square. Divide the chicken mixture between them equally, spooning it on top of the ham. Fold up the corners of the squares, pressing the edges together, but leaving a small opening at the top. Glaze the top of the pasties with the egg yolk. Grease a baking sheet and arrange the pasties on it. Bake at 200°C/400°F/gas 6 for 25 minutes. Remove from the oven and put 1 teaspoon of cream into the opening at the top of each. Serve at once.

Roast Chicken *(see overleaf)*

50 g/2 oz butter
2 chickens (850 g/1¾ lb each)
salt, pepper, paprika
1 kg/2 lb potatoes, cut into pieces

100 g/4 oz streaky bacon, chopped
250 g/9 oz shallots or small onions, chopped
5 tablespoons hot stock
sprigs parsley

Melt the butter in a roasting pan on top of the stove. Put in the chickens and brown for 10 minutes on all sides. Season well and continue frying for another 10 minutes, turning the chickens from time to time. Arrange the potatoes, bacon and shallots or onions around the chickens. Pour in the stock, cover the pan with aluminium foil, place in the oven and bake at 200°C/400°F/gas 6 for 40 minutes. Remove the foil from the pan and continue cooking for another 5 to 10 minutes, to brown the chickens. Arrange on a warmed serving dish and garnish with the parsley. Serve immediately.

Overleaf: roast chicken

69

Chicken with red wine sauce

Chicken with Red Wine Sauce

1·5 kg/3 lb chicken	150 g/5 oz mushrooms,
salt, pepper	quartered
100 g/4 oz butter	200 g/7 oz shallots, chopped
150 g/5 oz streaky bacon,	250 ml/8 fl oz red Bordeaux wine
chopped	

Divide the chicken into 4 portions and season with salt. Melt half the butter in a roasting pan on top of the stove. Add the chicken portions and brown on all sides for 10 minutes. Add the bacon, mushrooms and shallots to the pan and continue frying for 5 minutes. Cover the pan with aluminium foil and bake on the bottom shelf of the oven, at 200°C/400°F/gas 6, for 20 minutes. Arrange the chicken portions, bacon, mushrooms and shallots in a warmed dish and keep hot.

To make the sauce, add the wine to the juices in the pan. Bring to the boil, stirring. Strain through a sieve into a saucepan. Continue to boil the sauce until it has reduced by half. Divide the remaining butter into flakes. Using a wire whisk, whisk the butter flakes gradually into the sauce. Continue whisking the sauce until it is slightly foamy. Pour over the chicken and serve.

Goose Casserole

SERVES 6

1 goose breast	¼ celeriac root, chopped
2 tablespoons goose fat	250 g/9 oz carrots, chopped
2 goose legs	salt, pepper, dried marjoram
2 onions, chopped	600 ml/1 pint water
450 g/1 lb potatoes, chopped	1 tablespoon chopped parsley

Cut the goose breast into 4 portions. Put the fat into a frying pan and heat until very hot. Fry the goose portions (breast and legs) until crisp. Add the onions and fry until yellow. Put the goose portions and remaining chopped vegetables into a chicken brick or other clay pot, and season well with salt, pepper and marjoram. Pour in the water and cover with the lid. Place in a cold oven and bake at 220°C/425°F/gas 7 for 1½ hours, until tender. Take the clay pot out of the oven and carefully remove the bones from the goose legs. Sprinkle on the parsley and serve in the clay pot.

Note: If you do not have a chicken brick or similar clay pot, use an ordinary casserole, place in a preheated oven and reduce the cooking time to 1 hour.

Goose casserole

Duck Giblet and Bean Casserole

250 g/9 oz dried haricot or butter
  beans
1 litre/1¾ pints water
2 tablespoons oil
1 kg/2 lb duck giblets and wings
salt, dried thyme, dried
  marjoram, paprika
30 g/1¼ oz butter

2 leeks, sliced
2 onions, chopped
30 g/1¼ oz flour
1 tablespoon tomato purée
sugar
200 ml/6 fl oz red wine
sprig parsley

Soak the beans overnight in the water. Heat the oil in a large pan. Brown the duck giblets and wings on all sides for 5 minutes. Add the beans with the soaking water, and season with salt, thyme and marjoram. Bring to the boil, and simmer over gentle heat for about 1 hour. Add a little more hot water if necessary. Remove the duck giblets and wings from the pan and keep hot.

Melt the butter in a frying pan and gently fry the leeks and onions for 5 minutes. Sprinkle on the flour and continue frying for 1 minute, stirring. Stir this mixture into the beans and simmer for 7 minutes. Stir in the tomato purée, and season with paprika and a pinch of sugar. Remove the pan from the heat and stir in the wine. Remove the bones from the duck wings and cut up the giblets. Return the meat to the pan and adjust the seasoning. Simmer all the ingredients together gently for 5 minutes. Arrange in a warmed dish, garnish with the parsley, and serve immediately.

Duck giblet and bean casserole

Roast duck with chestnut stuffing

Roast Duck with Chestnut Stuffing

450 g/1 lb chestnuts	salt, pepper
40 g/1¼ oz butter	3 kg/6 lb duck
½ celeriac root, chopped	1 onion, chopped
600 ml/1 pint hot water	sprigs parsley

First, make the stuffing. Cut a cross in the chestnuts. Bring a pan of water to the boil, add the chestnuts and boil for 15 minutes. Then drain and peel them. Melt the butter in another pan and fry the celeriac for 5 minutes. Add 250 ml/8 fl oz of the hot water and the chestnuts, and season with salt. Simmer, covered, for 15 minutes, stirring from time to time.

Season the duck inside and out, and stuff it with the chestnut and celeriac mixture. Sew up the opening, and prick the skin of the duck all over with a needle. Place the duck in a roasting pan, cover with aluminium foil, and roast at 200°C/400°F/gas 6 for about 2 hours, or until tender. During the roasting time gradually add the remaining hot water, and baste the duck from time to time with the juices in the pan. Thirty minutes before the end of the cooking time add the onion to the pan. Ten minutes before the end of the cooking time remove the foil from the pan. This will allow the duck to brown.

Remove the duck from the pan, arrange on a warmed plate, and garnish with the parsley sprigs. Serve with croquette potatoes.

Roast Turkey *(see overleaf)*

1·5 kg/3 lb baby turkey	450 g/1 lb shallots or small
salt, pepper, dried thyme	onions
250 g/9 oz streaky bacon	750 g/1½ lb carrots, sliced
50 g/2 oz margarine	750 g/1½ lb small potatoes
	250 ml/8 fl oz hot stock

Season the turkey with salt, pepper and thyme, rubbing well into the skin. Place 3 or 4 slices of bacon over the turkey breast, and tie in place. Melt the margarine in a roasting pan on top of the stove, and brown the turkey for a few minutes on both sides. Place on the bottom shelf of the oven and roast at 220°C/425°F/gas 7 for 30 minutes. Turn the turkey from time to time, and baste with the juices in the pan.

Meanwhile, cut the remaining bacon into thin strips. Bring a pan of salted water to the boil, add the shallots or onions and simmer for 2 minutes. Remove and drain.

After 30 minutes' roasting time add the bacon, shallots or onions, carrots and potatoes to the roasting pan. Season with salt and pepper and pour in the stock. Replace on the bottom shelf of the oven and continue roasting, at 180°C/350°F/gas 4, for 1 hour. Remove from the oven and serve immediately.

Overleaf: roast turkey

75

Roast turkey with aubergines

Roast Turkey with Aubergines

2.5 kg/5 lb baby turkey
salt, pepper, chilli powder, mild
  paprika
75 g/3 oz margarine
250 ml/8 fl oz hot stock
2 aubergines

8 tomatoes
150 ml/¼ pint oil
450 g/1 lb mushrooms, thinly
  sliced
1 tablespoon chopped parsley
sprigs parsley

Season the inside of the turkey with salt and pepper. Melt the margarine in a roasting pan on top of the stove. Brown the turkey on all sides for 15 minutes. Pour in half the stock. Place the pan on the bottom shelf of the oven, and roast at 200°C/400°F/gas 6 for 2 hours. Baste frequently during the roasting time with the juices in the pan, gradually adding the rest of the stock.

While the turkey is roasting, prepare the vegetables. Cut off the stem ends of the aubergines, and cut them into slices about 1 cm/½ inch thick. Put them on a plate, sprinkle with salt, and let them stand for 30 minutes to draw out the juices. Cut out the hard parts near the stems of the tomatoes, and make a crossways cut at the bottom of each.

Ten minutes before the end of the roasting time add the tomatoes to the roasting pan. Heat 2 tablespoons of the oil in a frying pan, put in the mushrooms, season with salt and pepper, and fry gently for 8 minutes. Then mix in the chopped parsley, remove and keep hot. Rinse the aubergine slices under the cold tap and drain. Pat dry thoroughly with absorbent paper, and then sprinkle with pepper, chilli powder and paprika. Heat the remaining oil in another frying pan and fry the aubergine slices for 4 minutes each side. Remove and keep hot.

Take the roasting pan out of the oven, remove the turkey and arrange it on a warmed dish. Surround with the tomatoes, mushrooms and aubergines, and garnish with the parsley sprigs. Strain the juices from the roasting pan through a sieve into a saucepan. Reheat the juices and serve separately as a gravy.

78

Casserole of pheasant

Casserole of Pheasant

SERVES 3

1 hen pheasant	1 teaspoon sugar
salt	10 shallots or small onions
100 g/4 oz pork back fat, sliced	250 g/9 oz button mushrooms
40 g/1½ oz margarine	4 tablespoons Madeira
20 g/¾ oz butter	sprigs cress

Season the pheasant with salt. Tie the wings and legs to the body of the bird to form a neat shape, and cover with the slices of fat. Melt the margarine in a large flameproof casserole. Brown the pheasant on all sides for 5 minutes. Reduce the heat and continue frying for a further 15 minutes.

Meanwhile, melt the butter and sugar in a frying pan, and fry the onions until beginning to soften. Place the onions, with the mushrooms, round the pheasant. Cover the casserole and continue cooking for 30 minutes. Add the Madeira, heat through and serve, garnished with cress.

Pheasant with Apples and Chestnuts

250 g/9 oz chestnuts
250 ml/8 fl oz stock
1 tablespoon sugar
1 cock pheasant
salt, pepper
100 g/4 oz pork back fat, sliced
40 g/1½ oz margarine
250 ml/8 fl oz hot water

40 g/1½ oz butter
3 dessert apples, peeled, cored and cut into sixths
2 tablespoons Calvados
200 ml/6 fl oz cider
2 teaspoons cornflour
150 ml/¼ pint single cream
sprigs parsley

Cut a cross in the chestnut shells and place them on a baking sheet. Roast at 220°C/425°F/gas 7 for 15 minutes. Remove half the chestnuts from the oven and shell them, removing the brown inner skin as well as the outer shell. Then shell the remainder. (The chestnuts should be shelled in two batches; they are easier to deal with when hot.) Place the chestnuts and the stock in a saucepan, bring to the boil and simmer for 15 minutes, until almost all the liquid has boiled away. Add the sugar and continue cooking until the chestnuts are glazed. Put aside and keep hot.

Season the pheasant with salt. Tie the wings and legs to the body of the bird to form a neat shape, and cover with the slices of fat. Melt the margarine in a large flameproof casserole on top of the stove. Brown the pheasant well on all sides for 10 minutes. Then cover the casserole, place in the oven and cook at 170°C/325°F/gas 3 for 1 hour, or until tender. Add the hot water gradually, and baste the bird with the cooking liquid from time to time.

After 45 minutes' cooking time, melt the butter in a pan and gently fry the apples on all sides for 8 minutes. Set aside and keep hot.

Remove the casserole from the oven and transfer the pheasant to a warmed serving dish. Keep hot. Place the casserole on top of the stove and reheat the chestnuts and apples in the juices, reheating the chestnuts first. Arrange round the pheasant and keep hot.

To make the sauce, put the Calvados and cider into the casserole with the remaining juices, and bring to the boil. Mix the cornflour to a smooth paste in a cup with a little cold water. Blend a little of the hot sauce into the mixture, then return to the pan. Bring slowly to the boil, stirring constantly. Simmer for 2 to 3 minutes. Season with salt and a little pepper. Remove the pan from the heat and stir in the cream. Pour the sauce over the pheasant, chestnuts and apples, garnish with the parsley and serve.

Partridges Cooked in Bacon

SERVES 6

6 partridges (300 g/10 oz each)
salt, pepper
6 large slices pork back fat
100 ml/4 fl oz oil
350 g/12 oz carrots, cut into long pieces
2 onions, chopped

1½ teaspoons chopped parsley
1½ teaspoons dried sage
1½ teaspoons dried basil
500 ml/18 fl oz hot water
4 tablespoons brandy
1 tablespoon cornflour
250 ml/8 fl oz soured cream

Season the partridges with salt and pepper, inside and out. Cover the breast of each bird with a slice of fat, and tie in place with string. Heat the oil in a large roasting pan, and brown the partridges on all sides for 5 minutes. Add the carrots, onions, parsley, sage and basil to the pan, and continue frying for 3 minutes, stirring the vegetables. Pour in the water, cover the pan, and braise the partridges over gentle heat for 40 minutes.

Take the partridges out of the pan, and remove the string and slices of fat. Keep the partridges warm. Strain the pan juices through a sieve into a saucepan. Add the brandy. Mix the cornflour to a smooth paste in a cup with a little cold water. Blend a little of the hot liquid into the mixture, then return to the pan. Bring slowly to the boil, stirring constantly. Simmer for 2 to 3 minutes. Remove the pan from the heat and stir in the cream. Season to taste with salt and pepper and pour into a warmed sauceboat.

To serve, arrange the partridges on a warmed dish, and hand the sauce separately.

Right: partridges cooked in bacon
Below: pheasant with apples and chestnuts

Partridges with Bread Sauce

4 partridges (300g/10oz each)
salt, pepper
40g/1½oz pork back fat, thinly
  sliced
75g/3oz butter
250ml/8floz hot water
4 slices bread, crusts removed
sprigs cress
1 lemon, cut into eighths

BREAD SAUCE
500ml/18floz milk
1 onion
100g/4oz stale bread, crusts
  removed
30g/1¼oz butter
90ml/3½floz single cream
salt, cayenne, grated nutmeg
1 teaspoon lemon juice

Season the partridges with salt and pepper, inside and out.
Wrap the fat round them, and tie in place with string. Melt
50g/2oz of the butter in a roasting pan, and brown the
partridges on all sides for 5 minutes. Pour in the water, and
cook gently over low heat for 30 minutes.

Meanwhile, make the bread sauce. Bring the milk to the
boil in a pan with the onion. Crumble in the stale bread and
simmer gently for 5 minutes. Take out the onion. Sieve the
milk and the bread into a bowl. Stir in the butter and cream,
and season to taste with salt, cayenne, nutmeg and the lemon
juice. Keep hot.

Cut the slices of bread into triangles to make croûtons.
Melt the remaining butter in a frying pan and fry the croûtons
on both sides until golden brown. Remove and keep hot.

Remove the string and fat from the partridges, and cut the
birds in half. Arrange them on a warmed dish with the
croûtons. Serve, garnished with the cress and lemon wedges.
Hand the bread sauce separately.

Partridges with bread sauce

Stuffed pigeons

Stuffed Pigeons

100 g/4 oz stale bread, crusts
  removed
500 ml/18 fl oz hot stock
225 g/8 oz canned button
  mushrooms, drained
75 g/3 oz butter

2 onions, finely chopped
1 teaspoon chopped parsley
salt, pepper
4 pigeons (250 g/9 oz each)
juice ½ lemon
sprigs cress

To make the stuffing, crumble the bread into a bowl and pour on 150 ml/¼ pint of the stock. Cover and leave to soak for 15 minutes, and then squeeze out the stock. Chop 100 g/4 oz of the mushrooms.

Melt 10 g/⅓ oz of the butter in a pan. Add 1 of the chopped onions, the chopped mushrooms, the breadcrumbs and parsley. Season, and then fry gently for 5 minutes, stirring. Take the pan off the heat and allow to cool slightly.

Season the pigeons inside and out. Fill the birds with the stuffing and fasten the openings with cocktail sticks. Heat 40 g/1½ oz of the butter in a roasting pan, and brown the birds on all sides for 15 minutes. Pour in the rest of the stock. Cover the pan and braise the pigeons over low heat for 25 minutes.

After 15 minutes' cooking time melt the remaining butter in another pan. Add the remaining chopped onion, the whole mushrooms, and season. Fry gently for 5 minutes. Add the lemon juice and fry for a further 5 minutes.

Arrange the fried mushrooms and onion on a warmed dish. Remove the cocktail sticks from the pigeons, and lay them on top. Pour the juices from the pan over them. Serve, garnished with the cress.

Rolled shoulder of venison

Rolled Shoulder of Venison

SERVES 4–6

1 kg/2 lb boned shoulder of
  venison
salt, pepper
100 g/4 oz streaky bacon
40 g/1½ oz margarine
100 ml/4 fl oz hot water
150 ml/¼ pint red wine
2 onions, chopped

1 carrot, chopped
1 bay leaf
3 juniper berries, crushed
2 allspice berries
small piece lemon peel
1½ tablespoons cornflour
150 ml/¼ pint soured cream

Season the meat well with salt and pepper. Form the meat
into a roll shape, wrap the rashers of bacon round it, and tie
in place with string. Melt the margarine in a roasting pan on
top of the stove. Brown the joint on all sides for 10 minutes.
Then put into the oven and roast at 200°C/400°F/gas 6 for 1¼
hours, gradually adding the water and wine during cooking.
After 15 minutes' roasting time add onions, carrot, bay leaf,
juniper berries, allspice berries and lemon peel to the pan.

When the joint is cooked, take the pan out of the oven.
Remove the string from the joint, transfer it to a warmed
serving dish and keep hot. Strain the pan juices through a
sieve into a saucepan. Mix the cornflour to a smooth paste in
a cup with a little cold water. Blend a little of the hot sauce
into the mixture, then return to the pan. Bring slowly to the
boil, stirring constantly. Simmer for 2 to 3 minutes. Remove
the pan from the heat and stir in the cream. Serve the joint
with Brussels sprouts and mashed potatoes, and hand the
sauce separately.

Venison with Mushrooms

300 g/10 oz lean, tender venison
salt, pepper
300 g/10 oz mushrooms, sliced
100 g/4 oz margarine
1 onion, chopped
2 teaspoons prepared mustard

1 tablespoon flour
300 ml/½ pint meat stock
4 small potatoes, sliced
150 ml/¼ pint soured cream
1 teaspoon chopped parsley
1 teaspoon chopped chives

Cut the meat first into thin slices and then into strips. Season
the meat and the mushrooms. Melt 40 g/1½ oz of the
margarine in a frying pan and fry the onion until soft. Add
the meat and brown it, then add the mushrooms and
mustard. Sprinkle on the flour and stir well. Pour in the stock
and bring to the boil, stirring. Simmer for 20 minutes until all
the ingredients are tender.

Meanwhile, bring a pan of salted water to the boil. Add the
potato slices and simmer until almost cooked (about 10
minutes). Drain thoroughly. Melt the remaining margarine in
another frying pan, and fry the potatoes, turning frequently,
until crisp and golden. Remove from the pan and keep hot.

Remove the venison pan from the stove and stir in the
cream. Pour the mixture into a warmed serving dish, and
arrange the potatoes in the centre. Sprinkle on the parsley and
chives and serve.

Venison with mushrooms

Jugged hare

Rabbit casserole

Jugged Hare

SERVES 6

4 kg/9 lb oven-ready hare	200 g/7 oz streaky bacon, chopped
4 onions	1 stick celery, chopped
2 carrots	1 leek, chopped
8 black peppercorns	250 ml/8 fl oz hot stock
250 ml/8 fl oz red wine vinegar	salt
250 ml/8 fl oz red wine	1 tablespoon flour
2 tablespoons brandy	3 tablespoons redcurrant jelly

Divide the hare into 8 portions. Peel 2 of the onions and slice them into very thin rings. Cut 1 carrot into strips. Arrange the hare, onion rings, carrot strips and peppercorns alternately in a stoneware jar or bowl. Mix together the vinegar, wine and brandy and pour over the meat. Cover and leave to stand for 4 to 5 hours.

Fry the bacon in a large pan until the fat runs. Drain the hare portions, reserving the marinade liquid, and pat dry. Fry for 10 minutes with the bacon until browned on all sides. Chop the remaining carrot and onions, and add to the pan with the celery and leek. Fry for 5 minutes until lightly browned. Pour in the stock, season lightly with salt, cover the pan, and simmer for 1 hour until tender.

Transfer the hare portions to a warmed serving dish and keep hot. Strain the cooking liquid through a sieve into a saucepan, and bring to the boil. Mix together the flour, redcurrant jelly and 4 tablespoons of the reserved marinade liquid until smooth. Blend a little of the hot liquid into the mixture, then return to the pan. Bring slowly to the boil, stirring constantly. Simmer for 2 to 3 minutes. Pour this sauce over the hare and serve at once.

Rabbit Casserole

1.5 kg/3 lb oven-ready rabbit	150 g/5 oz canned button mushrooms, drained
salt, pepper	200 g/7 oz canned peas, drained
2 carrots, chopped	20 g/$\frac{3}{4}$ oz flour
3 onions, chopped	150 ml/$\frac{1}{4}$ pint sherry
1 leek, sliced	sprigs parsley
250 ml/8 fl oz hot stock	

Divide the rabbit into 8 portions. Grease a large ovenproof casserole with butter. Season the rabbit portions and place them in the casserole. Add the carrots, onions and leek. Season again and pour in the stock. Place the lid on the casserole and cook at 200°C/400°F/gas 6 for 1 hour 20 minutes. Add the mushrooms and peas to the casserole 20 minutes before the end of the cooking time.

Mix together the flour and sherry. Remove the casserole from the oven and stir in the flour and sherry mixture. Continue cooking, with the lid on, for another 5 minutes. Remove from the oven and serve, garnished with the parsley.

Vegetables

Vegetables

Vegetable and noodle hot-pot

Vegetable and Noodle Hot-pot

20 g/¾ oz butter
100 g/4 oz streaky bacon, chopped
1 large onion, chopped
450 g/1 lb potatoes, chopped
1 green pepper, seeded and chopped

1 red pepper, seeded and chopped
salt
3 teaspoons mild paprika
1.5 litres/2½ pints hot stock
250 g/9 oz curly ribbon noodles

Melt the butter in a flameproof casserole and fry the bacon until the fat runs. Add the onion and fry until golden. Add the potatoes and peppers, season with salt and the paprika, and pour in the stock. Bring to the boil. Reduce the heat and simmer for 20 minutes.

After 10 minutes bring a pan of salted water to the boil. Add the noodles and simmer for 8 minutes, or until just tender. Drain, rinse with boiling water, and drain again. Mix the noodles into the vegetable mixture and serve.

Vegetable casserole

Vegetable Casserole

20 g/$\frac{3}{4}$ oz butter	250 g/9 oz tomatoes, skinned,
100 g/4 oz streaky bacon,	seeded and quartered
chopped	salt, paprika
4 onions, chopped	$\frac{1}{2}$ teaspoon dried chervil
1 cucumber	$\frac{1}{2}$ teaspoon dried tarragon
1 red pepper, seeded and	1 teaspoon dried basil
chopped	150 ml/$\frac{1}{4}$ pint soured cream
	1 teaspoon chopped parsley

Melt the butter in a large pan and fry the bacon for 5 minutes. Add the onions and fry for another 5 minutes, until pale yellow. Meanwhile, peel the cucumber, cut it into quarters lengthways, and take out the seeds with a spoon. Chop the cucumber flesh.

When the onions are golden, add the cucumber, pepper and tomatoes to the pan. Cover and stew gently for 15 minutes. Season with salt, paprika, and the chervil, tarragon and basil. Finally, remove the pan from the heat and stir in the cream, together with the parsley. Reheat gently without boiling. Arrange in a warmed dish and serve at once, with French bread.

Lentils with prunes

Lentils with Prunes

375 g/13 oz lentils
1·7 litres/3 pints cold water
200 g/7 oz prunes
a few pieces bacon rind
1 stick celery, chopped
1 carrot, chopped
1 leek, chopped
salt, pepper
sugar
½ teaspoon dried thyme

3 tablespoons red wine vinegar
4 smoked sausages or ham
  sausages
1 tablespoon oil
75 g/3 oz streaky bacon,
  chopped
2 onions, chopped
1 teaspoon chopped parsley
sprig parsley

Soak the lentils overnight in 1·2 litres/2 pints of the water, and soak the prunes in the remaining water.

Next day, bring the lentils and soaking water to the boil in a pan with the bacon rind. Add the celery, carrot and leek, and simmer over gentle heat for 45 minutes. Meanwhile, in another pan, bring the prunes and soaking water to the boil, and simmer for 30 minutes. Then pour the juice from the prunes into the pan of lentils. Keep the prunes hot. Season the lentil mixture with salt, pepper, sugar, the thyme and the vinegar. Add the sausages to the pan, and simmer for another 20 minutes. Then take out the bacon rind.

Meanwhile, heat the oil in a pan and fry the bacon for 3 minutes. Add the onions and fry for another 3 minutes, until golden. Mix the bacon and onions with the lentils, and stir in the chopped parsley. Arrange the lentils in a warmed dish, placing the sausages on top. Put the prunes round the edge. Garnish with the parsley sprig and serve at once.

Lentil Casserole

375 g/13 oz lentils
1·2 litres/2 pints cold water
1 bay leaf
1 onion, chopped
salt, pepper
2 tablespoons oil
200 g/7 oz small onions
200 g/7 oz small carrots

20 g/¾ oz sugar
100 ml/4 fl oz stock
1 teaspoon chopped thyme
40 g/1½ oz butter
40 g/1½ oz flour
150 ml/¼ pint red wine
150 g/5 oz Parma ham, chopped

Soak the lentils overnight in the water.

Next day, place the lentils and soaking water, bay leaf and chopped onion in a pan. Season with salt. Bring to the boil and simmer over low heat for 1 hour, until tender.

After 30 minutes, heat the oil in another pan and fry the small onions and carrots for 5 minutes. Sprinkle on the sugar and continue cooking for another 3 minutes, until the sugar has caramelised. Add the stock and season with salt and the thyme. Bring to the boil and simmer for 20 minutes. Then mix with the lentils. Work the butter and flour together, and stir carefully into the lentil mixture. Season with salt and pepper, and continue to simmer gently for another 5 minutes, stirring from time to time.

Finally, stir in the wine and heat through. Place in a warmed bowl, scatter the ham on top, and serve immediately.

Lentil casserole

Bacon and Bean Casserole

375 g/13 oz dried haricot or
  butter beans
1.5 litres/2½ pints cold water
200 ml/6 fl oz red wine
375 g/13 oz streaky bacon, cut
  into pieces
2 cloves garlic
salt, pepper

375 g/13 oz potatoes, chopped
300 g/10 oz French beans,
  topped, tailed and cut into
  even lengths
4 tomatoes, skinned, seeded and
  chopped
1 teaspoon chopped parsley

Soak the dried beans overnight in the water.

Next day, place the beans and soaking water, wine and
bacon in a pan. Bring to the boil and simmer for 1 hour. Then
crush the garlic cloves with salt and add to the pan with the
potatoes. Season generously with salt and pepper, and
continue to simmer for another 10 minutes. Add the French
beans and simmer for a further 15 minutes. Add the tomatoes
to the casserole 5 minutes before the end of the cooking time.
Adjust seasoning to taste, stir in the parsley and serve.

French Bean Hot-pot

100 g/4 oz dried red kidney
  beans
100 g/4 oz dried haricot beans
1.5 litres/2½ pints cold water
1 clove garlic
salt, dried thyme
100 g/4 oz streaky bacon,
  chopped
1 onion, chopped

200 g/7 oz green French beans,
  topped, tailed and cut into
  even lengths
200 g/7 oz yellow French beans,
  topped, tailed and cut into
  even lengths
1 teaspoon chopped savory
1 teaspoon lemon juice

Soak the dried beans overnight in the water.

Next day, crush the garlic clove with salt. Fry the bacon in
a pan for 5 minutes, until the fat runs. Add the onion and
garlic, and fry for another 3 minutes. Then add the dried
beans with the soaking water, and season with thyme. Cover
the pan and simmer for 1½ hours, adding salt towards the end
of the cooking time. Add the French beans to the pan 20
minutes before the end of the cooking time. Stir in the savory
and lemon juice, and serve immediately.

*Left: bacon and bean
casserole*

*Right: French bean hot-
pot*

Stuffed onions

Stuffed Onions

30 g/1¼ oz butter
400 g/14 oz frozen kale
salt, pepper, grated nutmeg

4 large onions
20 g/¾ oz breadcrumbs

Melt 20 g/¾ oz of the butter in a pan. Add the kale, which should be slightly thawed, and simmer over a low heat for 1 hour. Add the seasonings and remove the pan from the heat.

Meanwhile, bring a pan of salted water to the boil. Add the onions and simmer for 20 minutes, until tender. Remove the onions from the pan, drain them, and allow to cool slightly. Then cut the top off each onion and scoop out most of the insides. Chop the scooped-out onion and the lids, chop the kale, and mix. Stuff the hollowed-out onions with this mixture. Grease an ovenproof dish and place the stuffed onions in it. Sprinkle the breadcrumbs over the tops of the onions. Divide the remaining butter into 4 pieces, and place 1 piece on top of each onion.

Place the dish on the top shelf of the oven and bake at 220°C/425°F/gas 7 for 15 minutes. Remove from the oven and serve at once.

Onions in wine

Onions in Wine

40 g/1½ oz butter
750 g/1½ lb onions, sliced
salt, pepper, dried thyme
sugar

juice ½ lemon
2 tablespoons flour
250 ml/8 fl oz white wine
1 teaspoon chopped parsley

Melt the butter in a pan and fry the onions for 10 minutes,
until golden. Season with salt, pepper, thyme, sugar and the
lemon juice. Sprinkle on the flour and fry for 2 minutes,
stirring carefully. Pour the wine into the pan, cover, and
simmer for 25 minutes. Transfer the onions to a warmed dish,
sprinkle on the parsley and serve.

Stuffed Baked Potatoes

SERVES 6

12 medium potatoes

CHEESE STUFFING

1 onion, chopped
100 g/4 oz cream cheese
1 teaspoon chopped chives
salt, pepper

FISH STUFFING

8 small canned herring fillets,
    drained
1 sprig each tarragon, dill,
    chervil and parsley, chopped

1 shallot, chopped
40 g/1½ oz butter
salt
lemon juice

SHRIMP STUFFING

40 g/1½ oz butter
2 hard-boiled egg yolks, mashed
½ teaspoon mustard powder
100 g/4 oz peeled shrimps

Scrub the potatoes, dry them and arrange on a baking sheet. Bake at 200°C/400°F/gas 6 for about 1 hour. Make the stuffings while the potatoes are baking (see below). When the potatoes are cooked take them out. Cut a cross in each potato, and peel back the skins to make flower-petal shapes. Scoop out a little of the potato inside. Divide the stuffings between the potatoes; each stuffing mixture should fill 4 medium potatoes.

Cheese stuffing: mix together the onion, cheese and chives until thoroughly blended. Season to taste.

Fish stuffing: roll up the herring fillets and place 2 inside each potato. Mix together the herbs and shallot, and work into the butter with a little salt and lemon juice. Place dabs of herb butter beside the rolled-up herring fillets.

Shrimp stuffing: mix together the butter, egg yolks and mustard powder. Place inside the potatoes and put the shrimps on top.

Stuffed baked potatoes

Potato cheese

Potato Cheese

1 kg/2 lb potatoes
200 g/7 oz Emmenthal cheese,
  grated
1 egg

500 ml/18 fl oz milk
salt
1 tablespoon chopped parsley
1 onion, chopped

Bring a pan of salted water to the boil. Add the potatoes and simmer them in their skins for 10 minutes. Drain the potatoes, skin them and cut into slices. Grease an ovenproof dish. Arrange the potato slices in layers, sprinkling grated cheese over each layer. Reserve 1 tablespoon of the grated cheese for the topping.

Beat together the egg and milk. Season with salt and stir in the parsley and onion. Pour this mixture over the potatoes and sprinkle the remaining cheese on top. Place the dish on the bottom shelf of the oven, and bake at 200°C/400°F/gas 6 for 45 minutes. Remove from the oven and serve.

Vichy Carrots

450 g/1 lb carrots
40 g/1½ oz butter
1 tablespoon castor sugar

salt, pepper
cold water as required

Cut the carrots into slices, or halve them lengthways. Leave young carrots whole. Melt 25 g/1 oz of the butter in a pan, add the carrots and sugar, and season. Pour in sufficient cold water to partly cover the carrots. Bring to the boil, cover, and simmer over low heat for 15 to 20 minutes, or until tender. Then remove the lid, increase the heat, and cook the carrots until all the water has evaporated, leaving just a little butter. Do not allow to brown. Transfer the carrots to a warmed dish and place the remaining butter on top. Serve immediately.

Braised Lettuce Hearts with Tomato Sauce

4 firm lettuces
150 g/5 oz thickly sliced streaky
  bacon
2 onions, sliced
2 carrots, thinly sliced
salt, pepper

250 ml/8 fl oz hot stock
20 g/¾ oz butter
1 tablespoon flour
1 tablespoon tomato purée
sugar
juice ½ lemon

Remove the outer leaves of the lettuces, and wash the lettuce hearts without taking them apart. Drain. Bring a pan of salted water to the boil and simmer the lettuce hearts for 2 minutes. Remove from the pan and drain well. Cut into quarters lengthways, removing the hard stalk if necessary. Squeeze the excess liquid out of the lettuce quarters and press them well together. Line an ovenproof casserole with the bacon slices. Arrange the onions and carrots over the bacon, and place the lettuce quarters on top. Season, and pour on the stock. Cover the casserole and cook at 200°C/400°F/gas 6 for 15 minutes.

Take the casserole out of the oven and lift out the lettuce quarters, leaving behind as much liquid as possible. Drain them and arrange on a warmed dish. Remove the carrots, onions and bacon, and place them round the lettuce quarters. Keep hot. Strain the cooking liquid through a sieve and keep it hot for making the sauce.

To make the sauce, melt the butter in a pan and sprinkle on the flour. Fry for 5 minutes, stirring, until lightly browned. Stir in the tomato purée and cook for a few more seconds. Then stir in the strained cooking liquid. Season with salt, pepper, sugar and the lemon juice. Bring to the boil and simmer for 5 minutes. Taste, adjust seasoning if necessary, and pour the sauce over the lettuce hearts. Serve at once.

Spinach with Eggs

3 tablespoons olive oil
1 clove garlic, finely chopped
1 kg/2 lb spinach, washed and
  picked over
salt, pepper, grated nutmeg

4 eggs
4 tablespoons single cream
20 g/¾ oz breadcrumbs
20 g/¾ oz butter, cut into flakes

Heat the oil in a pan and fry the garlic for 1 minute. Add the spinach, cover, and fry gently for 3 minutes. Season with salt, pepper and nutmeg. Beat the eggs and cream together and mix with the spinach. Grease an ovenproof dish and put the spinach mixture into it. Sprinkle on the breadcrumbs, and dot the top with butter. Bake at 220°C/425°F/gas 7 for 10 minutes. Remove from the oven and serve.

Left: braised lettuce hearts with tomato sauce

Below: spinach with eggs

Spinach with Mushrooms

75 g/3 oz butter
1 small onion, chopped
450 g/1 lb mushrooms, sliced
salt, pepper, grated nutmeg
juice ½ lemon
20 g/¾ oz flour

100 ml/4 fl oz hot stock
150 ml/¼ pint hot milk
450 g/1 lb frozen spinach
25 g/1 oz Emmenthal cheese,
  grated

Melt 20 g/¾ oz of the butter in a pan and fry the onion for 3 minutes, until it begins to soften. Add the mushrooms and fry for another 7 minutes. Season with salt, pepper and the lemon juice, and keep hot.

To make the sauce, melt 20 g/¾ oz of the butter in another pan. Stir in the flour a little at a time, and fry gently for 2 minutes. Slowly stir in the stock and the milk, bring to the boil, and simmer for 10 minutes. Strain the sauce. Season with salt and pepper, cover, and keep hot.

Melt the remaining butter in another pan. Add the frozen spinach, cover, and allow to thaw over gentle heat; this will take about 20 minutes. Stir the cheese into the spinach and continue cooking gently for 5 minutes, stirring from time to time. Mix the mushrooms and onions, and the sauce into the spinach. Season with salt and nutmeg. Reheat briefly without boiling. Arrange in a warmed dish and serve.

Steamed Broccoli

450 g/1 lb broccoli, broken into
  florets

1 teaspoon salt

Remove any coarse outer leaves or woody pieces of stem from the broccoli. Place the broccoli in a steamer over a pan of fast-boiling water. Sprinkle with the salt and cover the steamer with a tightly-fitting lid. Steam for 20 to 25 minutes, or until the florets are tender. Remove from the steamer, arrange in a warmed dish and serve immediately with hollandaise sauce (see below).

Hollandaise Sauce

MAKES 300 ml/½ pint

4 tablespoons white wine
  vinegar
4 egg yolks

200 g/7 oz butter, cut into pieces
salt, pepper
lemon juice

Boil the vinegar in a small pan until it has reduced by half, then allow to cool. Mix the cooled vinegar and egg yolks in a bowl. Place the bowl over a pan of boiling water, and whisk the egg yolks until they begin to thicken. Over a very low heat, whisk in the butter, a little at a time, until completely blended. Season, add lemon juice to taste, and serve immediately as an accompaniment to fish and vegetables.

Desserts

Apple and Currant Tart

300 g/10 oz flour	200 g/7 oz butter, cut into pieces
salt	100 g/4 oz currants
150 g/5 oz granulated sugar	750 g/1½ lb dessert apples, peeled,
2 teaspoons vanilla sugar	cored and sliced
1 egg	½ teaspoon ground cinnamon

Sift the flour and a pinch of salt into a mixing bowl. Make a well in the centre and add 100 g/4 oz of the granulated sugar, the vanilla sugar and egg. Scatter the butter round the edge of the flour. Working from the outside in, rub the ingredients together to make a smooth dough. Form into a ball, wrap in greaseproof paper, and allow to rest for 30 minutes in the refrigerator before use.

Grease a 25 cm/10 inch loose-based or spring clip tin. Roll out the pastry on a lightly floured surface and use to line the tin. Put the currants into a bowl and pour boiling water over them. Let them soak for 5 minutes, then drain and dry them. Arrange the apple slices in overlapping layers in the pastry case. Sprinkle them with the currants, remaining granulated sugar and the cinnamon. Bake at 220°C/425°F/gas 7 for 35 minutes. Remove from the oven, turn out and allow to cool. Serve with whipped cream.

Apple and currant tart

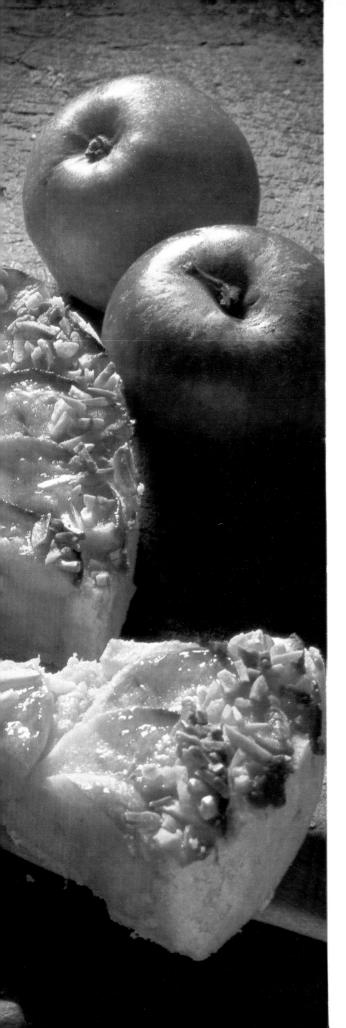

Baked Apple and Almond Flan

200 g/7 oz flour
salt
2 tablespoons cold water
150 g/5 oz butter, cut into pieces
450 g/1 lb apple purée

450 g/1 lb dessert apples, peeled, cored and sliced
100 g/4 oz apricot jam
3 tablespoons apricot brandy
75 g/3 oz chopped almonds

Sift the flour and a pinch of salt into a mixing bowl. Make a well in the centre and add the water. Scatter the butter round the edge of the flour. Working from the outside in, rub the ingredients together to make a smooth dough. Form into a ball, wrap in greaseproof paper, and allow to rest for 30 minutes in the refrigerator.

Grease a 23 cm/9 inch loose-based or spring clip tin. Roll out the pastry on a lightly floured surface and use to line the tin. Fill with the apple purée. Arrange the apple slices on top of the purée. Melt the apricot jam and apricot brandy together in a small pan. Paint over the apple slices with a pastry brush. Scatter the almonds round the edge and in the centre of the flan. Bake at 200°C/400°F/gas 6 for 30 minutes. Remove from the oven, turn out of the tin and allow to cool before serving.

Apple and Nut Pie

250 g/9 oz flour
150 g/5 oz sugar
salt
1 egg
125 g/4½ oz butter, cut into pieces

450 g/1 lb dessert apples, peeled, cored and sliced
50 g/2 oz ground hazelnuts
juice 1 lemon
1 teaspoon ground cinnamon

To make the pastry, sift the flour, 100 g/4 oz of the sugar and a pinch of salt into a mixing bowl. Make a well in the centre and add the egg. Scatter the butter round the edge of the bowl. Working from the outside in, rub the ingredients together to make a smooth dough. Cover and leave to rest for 30 minutes in the refrigerator.

Grease a 20 cm/8 inch pie dish. Roll out two-thirds of the pastry on a lightly floured surface and use to line the dish. Roll out the remaining pastry to make a lid.

To make the filling, mix the apples and hazelnuts in a bowl with the lemon juice, cinnamon and remaining sugar. Put into the pie dish. Prick the pastry lid several times with a fork and place over the filling. Bake at 220°C/425°F/gas 7 for 40 minutes. Take the pie out of the oven and allow to cool. Dust with icing sugar before serving.

Baked apple and almond flan

Strawberry meringue pudding

Apple Strudel

SERVES 6

450 g/1 lb flour
salt
50 g/2 oz butter, warmed
2 eggs
150 ml/¼ pint warm water
25 g/1 oz butter, melted

1 kg/2 lb cooking apples,
  peeled, cored and thinly sliced
75 g/3 oz sultanas
3 tablespoons fried breadcrumbs
75 g/3 oz granulated sugar
icing sugar

Sift the flour and a pinch of salt into a bowl. Make a well in the centre, and stir in the warmed butter, eggs and water with a palette knife. When mixed, knead the paste thoroughly until it no longer sticks to the hands, then cover and allow to stand. Spread a clean cloth on the table and sprinkle with flour. (The cloth should be approximately twice the size of a tea towel.) Roll out the dough on the cloth as thinly as possible. When it cannot be rolled any thinner, lift the dough on the back of the hands, and stretch it without breaking until it becomes as thin as tissue paper. Brush the pastry over with some of the melted butter.

To assemble the strudel, spread the apples over the dough. Sprinkle on the sultanas, breadcrumbs and granulated sugar. Fold the lower edge of the dough over the filling, then lift up the edge of the cloth and tilt, rolling up the strudel into a long roll. Trim the ends. Grease a baking sheet and cut the strudel into long pieces to fit it. Arrange on the baking sheet with the join underneath, and brush with the remaining melted butter. Bake at 200°C/400°F/gas 6 for about 30 minutes, until golden. Cut into portions and dust with icing sugar. Serve hot or cold.

Strawberry Meringue Pudding

450 g/1 lb strawberries, hulled
200 g/7 oz sugar
40 g/1½ oz flour
salt

3 eggs, separated
150 ml/¼ pint milk
grated rind ½ lemon

Cut any large strawberries in half. Place the strawberries in a bowl, sprinkle them with 25 g/1 oz of the sugar, cover, and leave to stand.

Meanwhile, make the pudding mixture. Sift the flour and a pinch of salt into a mixing bowl. Add the egg yolks and mix well. Gradually stir in the milk, followed by 25 g/1 oz of the sugar and the lemon rind. Thoroughly grease an ovenproof dish. Pour half of the pudding mixture into it, and place half of the strawberries on top. Then pour on the rest of the pudding mixture, and arrange the remaining strawberries on top. Bake at 200°C/400°F/gas 6 for 35 minutes.

Beat the egg whites until stiff and fold in the remaining sugar. Take the dish out of the oven and pile the meringue on top of the pudding. Replace in the oven and bake at the same temperature for another 10 minutes. Remove from the oven and serve immediately.

Almond and jam tart

Almond and Jam Tart

300 g/10 oz butter
200 g/7 oz granulated sugar
4 egg yolks
150 g/5 oz ground almonds
grated rind 1 lemon

300 g/10 oz flour
450 g/1 lb raspberry jam
25 g/1 oz blanched almonds, flaked
40 g/1½ oz icing sugar

In a large mixing bowl, cream the butter with 150 g/5 oz of the granulated sugar. Beat in 3 of the egg yolks, one at a time, until light and fluffy. Stir in the ground almonds, lemon rind and flour, and gather into a ball.

Grease a 25 cm/10 inch loose-based or spring clip tin, and sprinkle with 1 tablespoon of the granulated sugar. Roll out two-thirds of the pastry on a lightly floured surface and use to line the tin. Spread with the jam. Put the remaining pastry into a forcing bag with a star-shaped nozzle. Pipe a lattice pattern over the filling, and a border round the edge of the tart. Beat the remaining egg yolk and paint the lattice with it.

Place the tart on the bottom shelf of the oven and bake at 180°C/350°F/gas 4 for 1 hour. Take the tart out of the oven and remove from the tin. Decorate with the flaked almonds and dust with the icing sugar. Allow to cool before serving.

Walnut honey pie

Walnut Honey Pie

350 g/12 oz flour
125 g/4½ oz sugar
salt
grated rind ½ lemon
1 egg
150 g/5 oz butter, cut into pieces
1 egg yolk
1 tablespoon milk

FILLING
250 g/9 oz sugar
2 tablespoons clear honey
150 ml/¼ pint single cream
300 g/10 oz chopped walnuts
2 tablespoons kirsch

To make the pastry, sift the flour, sugar and a pinch of salt into a mixing bowl. Add the lemon rind, whole egg and butter, and rub together to make a smooth dough. Form into a ball, wrap in greaseproof paper and allow to rest for 30 minutes in the refrigerator.

Meanwhile, prepare the filling. Melt the sugar and honey together over gentle heat, stirring constantly. Remove the

pan from the heat and carefully stir in the cream. Reheat gently without boiling. Remove the pan from the heat again, and stir in the walnuts and kirsch. Allow to cool.

Take three-quarters of the pastry out of the refrigerator, leaving the remainder chilling. Roll out this pastry on a floured surface and use to line a 25 cm/10 inch loose-based or spring clip tin. Press the pastry well against the sides of the tin. Spread the cooled filling inside the pastry case and put the pie in the refrigerator to chill.

Roll out the remaining pastry thinly on the floured working surface, and cut into narrow strips. Use to make a lattice pattern on the pie, pressing the ends of the strips firmly against the sides of the pastry. Beat together the egg yolk and milk, and use to glaze the lattice. Bake at 200°C/400°F/gas 6 for 30 minutes. Cover the pie with greaseproof paper for the last 10 minutes of the cooking time. Take the pie out of the oven and allow to cool. Remove from the tin before serving.

Rhubarb tart

Rhubarb Tart

1 kg/2 lb rhubarb, cut into
  2·5 cm/1 inch pieces
525 g/1 lb 3 oz granulated sugar
100 g/4 oz butter
3 eggs
2 tablespoons white wine

250 g/9 oz flour
2 teaspoons baking powder
150 ml/¼ pint soured cream
1 teaspoon ground cinnamon
50 g/2 oz ground almonds
icing sugar

Put the rhubarb pieces into a bowl and sprinkle 400 g/14 oz of the granulated sugar over them. Cover and allow to stand for 1 hour. Meanwhile, cream the butter and 75 g/3 oz of the granulated sugar together until light and fluffy. Stir in 1 egg and the wine. Sift in the flour and baking powder, and stir into the other ingredients. Then, working from the outside in, knead the ingredients together to make a smooth dough. Form into a ball, wrap in greaseproof paper and allow to rest for 30 minutes in the refrigerator.

Grease a 25 cm/10 inch loose-based or spring clip tin. Roll out the pastry on a lightly floured surface and use to line the tin. Drain the rhubarb and arrange in the pastry case. Bake at 180°C/350°F/gas 4 for 40 minutes. Meanwhile, make the topping. Beat the cream and remaining eggs together, and stir in the remaining granulated sugar, the cinnamon and ground almonds. Mix thoroughly until smooth.

Take the tart out of the oven and pour the topping over it. Return to the oven and bake for another 25 minutes. Remove from the oven, turn out and dust with icing sugar. Allow to cool before serving.

Plum tart

Plum Tart

PASTRY
150 g/5 oz flour
100 g/4 oz ground almonds
100 g/4 oz sugar
salt
2 egg yolks
grated rind 1 lemon
150 g/5 oz butter, cut into pieces

FILLING
30 g/1¼ oz breadcrumbs
1 kg/2 lb dark-skinned plums,
   stoned
100 g/4 oz sugar
150 g/5 oz redcurrant jelly

Sift the dry ingredients for the pastry into a mixing bowl. Make a well in the centre and add the egg yolks and lemon rind. Scatter the butter round the edge. Working from the outside in, rub the ingredients together to make a smooth dough. Form into a ball, wrap in greaseproof paper, and allow to rest for 30 minutes in the refrigerator.

Grease a 25 cm/10 inch loose-based or spring clip tin. Roll out the pastry on a lightly floured surface and use to line the tin. Sprinkle the base of the tart with the breadcrumbs. Place the plums close together on the pastry, with the cut sides of the halves upwards. Bake at 180°C/350°F/gas 4 for 1 hour.

Remove the tart from the oven and turn out. Melt the redcurrant jelly in a small pan over gentle heat, stirring until smooth. Sprinkle the tart with the sugar and pour the redcurrant jelly over the top. Allow to cool before serving.

Bread and butter pudding

Bread and Butter Pudding

40 g/1½ oz butter
4 thick slices white bread
4 tablespoons brandy
3 eggs

250 ml/8 fl oz milk
60 g/2½ oz sugar
1 teaspoon ground cinnamon
100 g/4 oz chopped hazelnuts

Melt the butter in a pan and fry the bread on both sides, until golden. Grease an ovenproof dish and put the fried bread into it. Pour the brandy over the bread. Beat the eggs and milk together, pour into the dish, and leave to soak for about 15 minutes. Mix the sugar, cinnamon and chopped nuts, and scatter over the bread. Cover the dish with aluminium foil, and bake at 200°C/400°F/gas 6 for 30 minutes. Remove from the oven and serve hot.

Baked Custard

1 litre/1¾ pints milk
1 piece lemon rind
100 g/4 oz icing sugar

4 eggs, well beaten
20 g/¾ oz butter, cut into flakes
grated nutmeg

Put the milk and lemon rind into a pan, sift in the sugar, and bring to the boil, stirring. Take the pan off the heat and remove the lemon rind. Spoon the eggs gradually into the hot milk, stirring well.

Lightly grease an ovenproof soufflé dish. Pour the custard mixture into the dish and bake at 180°C/350°F/gas 4 for 45 minutes, or until set. When the custard starts to thicken, dot the top with the butter flakes and sprinkle with nutmeg. Remove from the oven when set and serve immediately.

Steamed Jam Pudding

225 g/8 oz flour
2 teaspoons baking powder
salt
100 g/4 oz butter, cut into pieces
100 g/4 oz castor sugar
1 egg, beaten

4–5 tablespoons milk
3 tablespoons red jam

SAUCE
4 tablespoons red jam
50 g/2 oz castor sugar
2 tablespoons water

Sift the flour, baking powder and a pinch of salt into a mixing bowl. Add the butter and rub in with the fingertips. Stir in the sugar. Mix together the egg and 4 tablespoons milk, and stir into the dry ingredients to make the mixture a soft, dropping consistency. Add the remaining tablespoon milk if necessary.

Grease a 1·2 litre/2 pint pudding basin and put the jam in the bottom. Pour the sponge mixture on top and cover the basin with greased greaseproof paper; fold a pleat in this to allow the pudding to rise during cooking. Fasten the paper with string. Place the pudding in a steamer over a pan of boiling water, and cover the steamer with a tightly-fitting lid. Steam for $1\frac{1}{2}$ to 2 hours, topping up the boiling water as necessary to prevent the pan boiling dry.

About 10 minutes before the pudding is cooked, prepare the sauce. Put the jam, sugar and water into a small pan. Stir over gentle heat until the sugar dissolves, then bring to the boil. Simmer for 2 to 3 minutes, stirring, until the sauce is syrupy. Pour into a warmed sauceboat and keep hot.

Remove the pudding from the steamer. Remove the paper and loosen the sides of the pudding with a palette knife. Turn out on to a warmed dish. Serve immediately, with the jam sauce.

Queen of Puddings

100 g/4 oz breadcrumbs
50 g/2 oz butter
grated rind 2 lemons
150 g/5 oz castor sugar

600 ml/1 pint milk
2 eggs, separated
5 tablespoons strawberry jam
1 egg white

Place the breadcrumbs, butter, lemon rind and 50 g/2 oz of the sugar in a bowl. Heat the milk gently and pour over the dry ingredients. Leave to soak for 30 minutes, and then stir in the egg yolks. Grease a soufflé dish and pour in the mixture. Bake at 180°C/350°F/gas 4 for 45 minutes, or until set.

When the pudding is set, spread the jam on top. Whisk the 3 egg whites until stiff. Stir in 25 g/1 oz of sugar and whisk again until very stiff. Then lightly stir in the rest of the sugar. Spread the meringue over the pudding and bake at 200°C/400°F/gas 6 until set and golden brown. Remove from the oven and serve immediately.

Breads and Cakes

Cottage Loaf

30 g/1¼ oz fresh yeast or 15 g/½ oz
  dried yeast
1 teaspoon sugar
500 ml/18 fl oz warm milk
1 kg/2 lb strong white flour
2 teaspoons salt

100 g/4 oz lard or margarine
2 eggs (optional)

GLAZE
1 egg, beaten
1 tablespoon milk

To make the dough, cream the fresh yeast with the sugar and a little of the milk, then add the remaining milk. (If using dried yeast, dissolve the sugar in the milk, sprinkle on the yeast and stir well.) Leave to stand in a warm place for about 10 minutes.

Meanwhile sift the flour and salt into a bowl. Rub the fat into the flour. Make a well in the centre and pour in the yeast mixture, and the eggs if used. Working from the outside in, knead to a soft dough which leaves the sides of the bowl clean (about 10 minutes). Add a little more flour if necessary. Allow the dough to stand in a warm place, covered with a clean cloth, until it has doubled in size.

Turn the dough on to a floured surface. Knead again for 1 to 2 minutes to knock out air bubbles. Cut off two-thirds of the dough and make into a bun shape. Make the remaining third into another, smaller, bun shape. Place the smaller one on top of the larger one, and secure by putting your little finger through the centre. Grease a baking sheet and place the loaf on it. Cover with a clean cloth and leave to prove until the dough has doubled in size.

Mix together the beaten egg and milk for the glaze and brush over the loaf. Bake at 220°C/425°F/gas 7 for 45 minutes to 1 hour, or until cooked through and golden brown. Remove from the oven and allow to cool.

Plaited Milk Loaves

MAKES 3

15 g/½ oz fresh yeast or 2
  teaspoons dried yeast
½ teaspoon sugar
300 ml/½ pint warm milk
450 g/1 lb strong white flour
1 teaspoon salt

50 g/2 oz lard or margarine
1 egg (optional)

GLAZE
1 egg, beaten
1 tablespoon milk

To make the dough, cream the fresh yeast with the sugar and a little of the milk, then add the remaining milk. (If using dried yeast, dissolve the sugar in the milk, sprinkle on the yeast and stir well.) Leave to stand in a warm place for about 10 minutes.

Meanwhile sift the flour and salt into a bowl. Rub the fat into the flour. Make a well in the centre and pour in the yeast mixture, and the egg if used. Working from the outside in, knead to a soft dough which leaves the sides of the bowl clean (about 10 minutes). Add a little more flour if necessary. Allow the dough to stand in a warm place, covered with a clean cloth, until it has doubled in size.

Turn the dough on to a floured surface. Knead again for 1 to 2 minutes to knock out air bubbles. Divide the dough into three, and roll each piece of dough into a piece 50 cm/20 inches long. The pieces should be thinner at the ends than in the middle. Plait the three lengths of dough and curl each one round into a decorative shape as shown in the picture (see page 115). Grease a large baking sheet and place the loaves on it. Cover with a clean cloth and leave to prove until the dough has doubled in size.

Mix together the beaten egg and milk for the glaze and brush over the loaves. Bake at 220°C/425°F/gas 7 for 20 to 30 minutes, until golden brown. Remove from the oven and allow to cool.

Plaited milk loaf

Brioches

MAKES 20—24

15 g/$\frac{1}{2}$ oz fresh yeast or 2
    teaspoons dried yeast
25 g/1 oz castor sugar
2—3 tablespoons warm water
450 g/1 lb strong white flour
$\frac{1}{2}$ teaspoon salt

175 g/6 oz margarine
4 eggs

GLAZE

1 egg, beaten
1 tablespoon milk

To make the dough, cream the fresh yeast with $\frac{1}{2}$ teaspoon of
the sugar and a little of the water, then add the remaining
water. (If using dried yeast, dissolve $\frac{1}{2}$ teaspoon of the sugar in

Muffins

30 g/1¼ oz fresh yeast or 15 g/½ oz
  dried yeast
1 teaspoon sugar
250 ml/8 fl oz warm milk
450 g/1 lb strong white flour

salt
40 g/1½ oz butter, cut into pieces

GLAZE
1 egg, beaten
1 tablespoon milk

To make the dough, cream the fresh yeast with the sugar and a little of the milk, then add the remaining milk. (If using dried yeast, dissolve the sugar in the milk, sprinkle on the yeast and stir well.) Leave to stand in a warm place for about 10 minutes.

Meanwhile sift the flour and a pinch of salt into a bowl. Rub in the butter. Make a well in the centre and pour in the yeast mixture. Working from the outside in, knead to a soft dough which leaves the sides of the bowl clean (about 10 minutes). Add a little more flour if necessary. Allow the dough to stand in a warm place, covered with a clean cloth, until it has doubled in size.

Turn the dough on to a floured surface. Knead again for 1 to 2 minutes to knock out air bubbles. Roll out the dough to a thickness of 1 cm/½ inch, and cut into 7·5 cm/3 inch rounds. Re-roll and cut the dough until all is used up. Grease a baking sheet and place the muffins on it. Cover with a clean cloth and leave to prove for 20 minutes.

Mix together the beaten egg and milk for the glaze, and brush over the muffins. Place the baking sheet on the bottom shelf of the oven and bake at 200°C/400°F/gas 6 for 20 minutes. Remove from the oven and serve while still warm, with butter.

Brioches

the water, sprinkle on the yeast and stir well.) Leave to stand in a warm place for about 10 minutes.

Meanwhile sift the flour, salt and remaining sugar into a bowl. Rub in the margarine. Make a well in the centre and pour in the yeast mixture and eggs. Working from the outside in, and adding more warm water if necessary, knead to a soft dough, which leaves the sides of the bowl clean (about 10 minutes). Allow the dough to stand in a warm place, covered with a clean cloth, until it has doubled in size.

Turn the dough on to a floured surface. Knead again for 1 to 2 minutes to knock out air bubbles. Take two-thirds of the

dough and divide it into 20 to 24 large balls. Divide the remaining third into 20 to 24 small balls. Grease sufficient brioche moulds or patty tins. Place a large ball in each mould or tin, and flatten slightly. Make a small hole in the top, dampen it and fix a small ball firmly on top. Cover with a clean cloth and leave to prove for 20 minutes.

Mix together the beaten egg and milk for the glaze, and brush over the brioches. Arrange the brioche moulds on baking sheets. Bake at 220°C/425°F/gas 7 for 15 to 20 minutes, until golden brown. Take out of the oven, remove from the brioche moulds or patty tins, and allow to cool.

Swedish bread

Meanwhile sift the flour, salt, cinnamon and remaining granulated sugar into a bowl. Rub in the butter. Make a well in the centre and pour in the yeast mixture and egg. Working from the outside in, knead to a soft dough which leaves the sides of the bowl clean (about 10 minutes). Add a little more flour if necessary. Allow the dough to stand in a warm place, covered with a clean cloth, until it has doubled in size.

Turn the dough on to a floured surface. Knead again for 1 to 2 minutes to knock out air bubbles. Divide the dough into two, and make each piece into a loaf 20 cm/8 inches long. Make several diagonal cuts on top of each loaf. Grease a baking sheet and place the loaves on it. Cover with a clean cloth and leave to prove for 20 minutes.

Mix together the beaten egg, water and a pinch of salt for the glaze, and brush over the loaves. Sprinkle them with the coarse sugar and nuts. Bake at 220°C/425°F/gas 7 for 20 to 30 minutes, until golden brown. Remove from the oven and allow to cool.

Herb Bread

40 g/1½ oz fresh yeast or 20 g/¾ oz dried yeast	1 teaspoon chopped parsley
1 teaspoon sugar	2 teaspoons chopped chives
250 ml/8 fl oz warm water	1 tablespoon caraway seeds
250 g/9 oz strong white flour	1 tablespoon fennel seeds
250 g/9 oz rye flour	1 tablespoon dried basil
1 tablespoon salt	75 g/3 oz butter, cut into pieces
1 teaspoon chopped dill	
	GLAZE
	50 g/2 oz butter, melted

To make the dough, cream the fresh yeast with the sugar and a little of the water, then add the remaining water. (If using dried yeast, dissolve the sugar in the water, sprinkle on the yeast and stir well.) Leave to stand in a warm place for about 10 minutes.

Meanwhile sift both flours, the salt and all the herbs into a bowl. Rub in the butter. Make a well in the centre and pour in the yeast mixture. Knead to a soft dough which leaves the sides of the bowl clean (about 10 minutes). Add a little more flour if necessary. Allow the dough to stand in a warm place, covered with a clean cloth, until it has doubled in size.

Turn the dough on to a floured surface. Knead again for 1 to 2 minutes to knock out air bubbles. Form the dough into a long loaf shape. Make diagonal cuts along the top with a knife. Grease a baking sheet and place the loaf on it. Cover with a clean cloth and leave to prove for 30 minutes.

Paint half of the melted butter over the loaf and bake at 220°C/425°F/gas 7 for 1 hour, until golden brown. Paint the rest of the butter over the loaf 10 minutes before the end of the cooking time. Remove from the oven and allow to cool.

Swedish Bread

MAKES 2

50 g/2 oz fresh yeast or 25 g/1 oz dried yeast	GLAZE
175 g/6 oz granulated sugar	1 egg beaten
500 ml/18 fl oz warm milk	2 tablespoons water
1 kg/2 lb strong white flour	salt
½ teaspoon salt	25 g/1 oz coarse sugar
2 teaspoons ground cinnamon	30 g/1¼ oz chopped almonds
200 g/7 oz butter, cut into pieces	
1 egg	

To make the dough, cream the fresh yeast with 2 teaspoons of the granulated sugar and a little of the milk, then add the remaining milk. (If using dried yeast, dissolve 2 teaspoons of the granulated sugar in the milk, sprinkle on the yeast and stir well.) Leave to stand in a warm place for about 10 minutes.

Herb bread

Parkin

250 g/9 oz flour
250 g/9 oz oatmeal
2 teaspoons baking powder
2 teaspoons ground ginger
125 g/4½ oz sugar

60 g/2½ oz butter, cut into pieces
60 g/2½ oz lard, cut into pieces
350 g/12 oz golden syrup
4 tablespoons milk

Sift the flour, oatmeal, baking powder, ginger and sugar into a bowl. Add the fats and rub them in. Stir in the syrup and milk gradually, and mix to a fairly stiff consistency. Allow to rest for 30 minutes in the refrigerator.

Grease a tin 25 × 20 × 4 cm/10 × 8 × 1½ inches, and line it with greased greaseproof paper. Turn the mixture into the tin and bake at 180°C/350°F/gas 4 for about 45 minutes, or until the mixture shrinks slightly from the sides of the tin. Remove from the oven and cool slightly. Then turn out of the tin, remove the lining paper and cool on a wire rack. Serve cut in thick slices.

Parkin

Cherry Sponge

200 g/7 oz butter	2 tablespoons milk
175 g/6 oz castor sugar	1 tablespoon breadcrumbs
1 tablespoon vanilla sugar	850 g/1¾ lb stoned morello
salt	cherries
3 eggs	20 g/¾ oz granulated sugar
200 g/7 oz flour	20 g/¾ oz chopped almonds
2 teaspoons baking powder	

Cream the butter in a bowl. Gradually mix in the castor sugar, vanilla sugar and a pinch of salt. Beat in the eggs, one at a time. Fold in the flour and baking powder. Then add the milk, a little at a time. Grease a 25 cm/10 inch loose-based or spring clip tin. Sprinkle the base with the breadcrumbs. Pour in the cake mixture and level the top. Cover with the cherries. Bake at 180°C/350°F/gas 4 for 40 minutes to 1 hour.

Mix the granulated sugar and chopped almonds, and sprinkle over the cake 10 minutes before the end of the cooking time. Remove the cake from the oven and cool slightly. Then turn out and cool on a wire rack.

Cherry sponge

Dundee cake

Dundee Cake

225 g/8 oz butter	60 g/2½ oz candied peel, chopped
225 g/8 oz sugar	75 g/3 oz glacé cherries
6 eggs	75 g/3 oz ground almonds
225 g/8 oz flour	grated rind 1 orange
100 g/4 oz currants	15 g/½ oz flaked almonds,
100 g/4 oz seedless raisins	chopped
100 g/4 oz sultanas	

Cream the butter and sugar until light and fluffy. Gradually beat in the eggs, one at a time. Fold in the flour. Then fold in the dried fruit, ground almonds and orange rind.

Line a rectangular cake tin 23 cm/9 inches long with greased greaseproof paper. Spoon in the cake mixture and level the top. Scatter the chopped almonds evenly over the cake mixture. Place the tin on the bottom shelf of the oven and bake at 150°C/300°F/gas 2 for 2½ hours. Remove from the oven and allow to cool slightly before turning out. Peel off the paper and cool the cake on a wire rack.

Saffron Cake

40 g/1½ oz fresh yeast or 20 g/¾ oz
  dried yeast
50 g/2 oz granulated sugar
150 ml/¼ pint warm milk
450 g/1 lb strong white flour
salt, powdered saffron
grated rind ½ lemon
1 tablespoon vanilla sugar

125 g/4½ oz butter, cut into pieces
125 g/4½ oz lard, cut into pieces
1 tablespoon hot water
100 g/4 oz candied lemon peel,
  finely chopped
300 g/10 oz currants
200 g/7 oz seedless raisins

GLAZE
100 g/4 oz butter, melted

To make the dough, cream the fresh yeast with 1 teaspoon of
the granulated sugar and a little of the milk, then add the
remaining milk. (If using dried yeast, dissolve 1 teaspoon of
the granulated sugar in the milk, sprinkle on the yeast and stir
well.) Leave to stand in a warm place for about 10 minutes.

Meanwhile sift the flour, a pinch of salt, the remaining
granulated sugar, the lemon rind and vanilla sugar into a
bowl. Rub in the fats. Make a well in the centre and pour in
the yeast mixture. Infuse a pinch of saffron in the hot water,
and add to the mixture with the dried fruit. Working from the
outside in, knead to a soft dough which leaves the sides of the
bowl clean (about 10 minutes). Add a little more flour if
necessary. Allow the dough to stand in a warm place, covered
with a clean cloth, until it has doubled in size.

Grease a rectangular tin 30 cm/12 inches long and put the
dough into it. Place on the bottom shelf of the oven and bake
at 200°C/400°F/gas 6 for 1 hour. After 40 minutes' baking
time brush the cake with the melted butter and return to the
oven for the final 20 minutes. Take the cake out of the oven
and cool slightly before turning out on to a wire rack.

Saffron cake

Queen Elizabeth cake

Queen Elizabeth Cake

100 g/4 oz stoned dried dates,
  chopped
150 g/5 oz flour
100 g/4 oz butter
75 g/3 oz chopped walnuts
150 g/5 oz granulated sugar

1 teaspoon baking powder
½ teaspoon salt
1 egg, well beaten
1 teaspoon vanilla essence
150 g/5 oz soft brown sugar
2 tablespoons single cream

Pour boiling water over the dates and leave them to soak.
Meanwhile, sift the flour into a bowl. Add 60 g/2½ oz of the
butter and rub in. Then stir in half the walnuts, the
granulated sugar, baking powder and salt. Drain the dates,
mix with the egg and vanilla essence, and stir thoroughly into
the flour mixture.

Line a rectangular cake tin 20 × 10 cm/8 × 4 inches with
greased greaseproof paper. Put the cake mixture into the tin
and level the top. Place on the bottom shelf of the oven and
bake at 200°C/400°F/gas 6 for 1 hour. Take the cake out of
the oven, turn it out of the tin, peel off the paper, and cool
on a wire rack.

To make the icing, put the remaining butter, the brown
sugar and cream into a bowl. Stir over a pan of hot water
until you have a thick, creamy mixture. Spread over the
cooled cake and scatter the remaining walnuts on top.

Angel cake

Angel Cake

10 egg whites
325 g/11 oz castor sugar
1 tablespoon vanilla sugar
grated rind $\frac{1}{2}$ lemon
165 g/5$\frac{1}{2}$ oz flour

$\frac{1}{2}$ teaspoon cream of tartar
salt
3 tablespoons lemon juice
150 g/5 oz icing sugar
candied orange and lemon slices

Beat the egg whites until stiff. Fold in the castor sugar, vanilla
sugar and lemon rind. Sift the flour, cream of tartar and a
pinch of salt, and fold lightly into the egg-white mixture.
Grease a 20 cm/8 inch loose-based or spring clip tin and fill
with the cake mixture. Bake at 180°C/350°F/gas 4 for 45
minutes to 1 hour. Take the cake out of the oven and turn out
of the tin. Allow to cool.

To make the icing, mix the lemon juice and icing sugar and
spread over the cake. Decorate with the candied orange and
lemon slices.

Index